DATE DUE

JAMES BOSWELL

James Boswell

By A. RUSSELL BROOKS

Kentucky State College

Twayne Publishers, Inc.   ::   New York

To
Sara

Preface

Critics from Boswell's time to the present have had at their disposal great quantities of material from which they could attempt to show either that James Boswell was more fool than artist or that, whether he was a fool or not, he was assuredly an artist. Contenders for both viewpoints have cited evidence from *The Life of Samuel Johnson, LL.D.*; several other books; numerous shorter publications; and many letters, periodical essays, poems, and miscellaneous items. Since discovery in the middle of the nineteenth century of his letters to the Reverend William Johnson Temple and others and, in the 1920's and 1930's, of hoards of private documents hidden away in Scottish and Irish castles, materials for estimating him as writer and man have collected into a formidable mass and have thus become a treasure and a challenge to critics, literary historians, and biographers.

Students of Boswell remain perplexed by contradictions in his personality, but the new evidence has afforded the basis for reconciling them and thus arriving at a truer, if less simple, picture of the man in relation to his art and to the crosscurrents of his age. Any view of him which fails to acknowledge his exceptional gifts and his deliberate artistry is obsolescent. Since discovery of his personal documents, we can see him at work carefully considering method in relation to ends desired and shaping his materials in accordance with a thoughtfully worked-out theory of biographical representation. The relation between the Journals and the *Life* has been ably shown by Geoffrey Scott in Volume VI of *The Private Papers of James Boswell* (18 vols., 1928-33) and by Professor Pottle and his Yale associates in their preparation of the trade editions of the Boswell documents. Aside from their thoroughgoing commentaries, only a few thoughtful readings of the Journals have come forth.

This study is not concerned to prove, by comparing Boswell's biography of Johnson with other great biographies or by any other means, that Boswell remains preeminent among biographers. Here his superiority is universally recognized, and he may never be dislodged from his niche. It is also outside the scope of this volume to do more than merely mention his effect on subsequent biography. He had a long and productive career as a writer, yet aside from his two books on Johnson and one on Corsica, he was hardly considered a distinguished author in his own day. His fame independent of Johnson was, for the most part, achieved posthumously—in the publication of his London Journal (1762-63), travel accounts, and other Journals.

An attempt is made here to provide a fuller view of Boswell's career as a writer than heretofore has been encompassed in a single study and to emphasize the unique coalescence of his personal experiences with his artistic outlook. His preference for things English made him critical of his own country. He thus experienced an inner conflict throughout his life, which shaped his personality and affected the substance and style of his unpublished and published writings. Recognition of this struggle can facilitate our understanding of some of the impulses that issued in the dual achievement of the fullest biography ever written and the most complete story of one's own adult life. The former, in a modified sense, is a part of the latter. A knowledge of Boswell and of his life story is by no means essential to an understanding of Johnson, but it is indispensable for a sound estimate of Boswell's biography of Johnson. Consideration will therefore be given in this study to his unique achievement in the area of autobiographical writing (particularly his Journal), which is receiving increased attention but still far too little recognition.

A. RUSSELL BROOKS

Kentucky State College
Frankfort, Kentucky

Acknowledgments

I wish to thank McGraw-Hill Book Company and the Boswell Papers Editorial Committee of Yale University for permission to quote from the eighteen-volume limited edition of the Private Papers of James Boswell, the Yale Editions of the Boswell Papers, and *Journal of a Tour to the Hebrides*, edited by Frederick A. Pottle and Charles H. Bennett (New York, 1936); the Clarendon Press for permission to quote from the Hill-Powell six-volume edition of Boswell's *Life of Samuel Johnson* (Oxford, 1934-50); and the Stanford University Press for permission to quote from Margery Bailey's two-volume edition of Boswell's "Hypochondriack" essays (Stanford, 1928). I am grateful to Professor Pottle and the staff of the Boswell Office, Yale University Library, for their kind cooperation on a number of occasions; to Miss Sylvia Bowman, editor of the Twayne's English Authors Series, for invaluable suggestions; to the Southern Fellowships Fund for a research fellowship that enabled me to complete this study; to Kentucky State College for sabbatical leave; and to Miss Jacqueline Pettiford and Mrs. Judith H. Ward for their extraordinary resourcefulness and proficiency in typing the manuscript.

Contents

Chronology

1740   James Boswell born in Edinburgh.

1753- Took undergraduate arts course at College of Edinburgh
1758   (University of Edinburgh).

1758   "An Evening Walk in the Abbey-Church of Holyroodhouse," his first poem to be printed (in *Scots Magazine*).

1758- Studied law at the University of Edinburgh.
1759

1759   Matriculated at the University of Glasgow to study civil law, where he attended Adam Smith's lectures in philosophy and belles lettres.

1760   Left the University of Glasgow in the spring for his first visit to London. Became Roman Catholic, but was quickly persuaded by the earl of Eglington to give up Roman Catholicism.

1760   Published anonymously *Observations, Good or Bad, Stupid or Clever, Serious or Jocular, on Squire Foote's Dramatic Entertainment, entitled, The Minor. By a Genius.*

1761   Collaborated with Andrew Erskine and George Dempster in anonymous publication of *An Elegy on the Death of an Amiable Young Lady with an Epistle from Menalcas to Lycidas, to which are prefixed Three Critical Recommendatory Letters.*

1761   Published anonymously *An Ode to Tragedy.*

1762   Collaborated with Andrew Erskine and others in publication of the second volume of *A Collection of Original Poems by Scotch Gentlemen.*

1762   Published anonymously the poem *The Cub at New-Market.*

1762- Second visit to London. Met Samuel Johnson.
1763

1763   Collaborated with Andrew Erskine and George Dempster in anonymous publication of *Critical Strictures on the New*

Tragedy of Elvira written by David Mallock.

1763   Collaborated with Andrew Erskine in publication of *Letters between The Honourable Andrew Erskine, and James Boswell, Esq.* Name on a title page for first time.

1763   To Utrecht to study civil law.

1764- Grand tour of Europe: Holland, Germany, Switzerland, Italy,
1766   Corsica, and France. Formed acquaintances with Voltaire, Rousseau, and Paoli.

1766   Mother died.

1766   Returned from European tour.

1766   Published law thesis, *Disputation Juridica.* Admitted to Scottish bar; began law practice in Edinburgh.

1767   Edited *The Essence of the Douglas Cause.* Assisted in editing *Letters of the Right Honourable Lady Jane Douglas.* Published poem, (broadside) *The Douglas Cause*, and an allegory on the Douglas case, *Dorando, A Spanish Tale.*

1768   First important book: *An Account of Corsica, the Journal of a Tour to that Island; and the Memoirs of Pascal Paoli.* First edition, Glasgow; second edition, London.

1769   Edited *British Essays in Favour of the Brave Corsicans.*

1769   Participated in the Stratford Shakespeare Jubilee, published broadside: *Verses in the Character of a Corsican at Shakespeare's Jubilee, Stratford-Upon-Avon, Sept. 6, 1769.*

1769   Married Margaret Montgomery.

1770   First son born; died almost immediately.

1770   *On the Profession of a Player*, a series of three essays in the *London Magazine.*

1771   Wrote dedication to David Garrick for Donaldson's second edition of *The Works of Shakespeare.*

1772   *Reflections on the Late Alarming Bankruptcies in Scotland.* "A Sketch of the Constitution of Scotland," in *Scots Magazine.*

1773   Daughter Veronica born.

1773   Elected member of the Literary Club.

1773   Toured Hebrides with Johnson.

1774   *Decision of the Court of Session on Literary Property.*

1774   Daughter Euphemia born.

1774   Published in *Scots Magazine* and *London Magazine* accounts of the travels of James Bruce.

1775 Son Alexander born.

1776 Son David born.

1777- *The Hypochondriack*, series of seventy monthly essays in the
1783 *London Magazine*.

1778 Son James born.

1782 Father died.

1783 *A Letter to the People of Scotland on the Present State of the Nation.*

1784 Published anonymously *Ode by Samuel Johnson to Mrs. Thrale, Upon their Supposed Approaching Nuptials.*

1784 Samuel Johnson died.

1785 *A Letter to the People of Scotland, on the Alarming Attempt to Infringe the Articles of Union, and introduce a Most Pernicious Innovation, by Diminishing the Number of Lords of Session.*

1785 *Journal of a Tour to the Hebrides.*

1786 Admitted to the English bar. Moved family to London.

1786 Elected Recorder of Carlisle.

1790 Broadside: *William Pitt, the Grocer of London.*

1791 *The Life of Samuel Johnson, LL.D.*

1791 Published *Memoirs.*

1791 *No Abolition of Slavery; or the Universal Empire of Love: A Poem.*

1793 Published *Corrections and Additions* to the *Life.*

1795 Died in London, May 19.

CHAPTER 1

At the Crossroads

T HE chief significance of Boswell's Scotch-English tension in relation to his life as a creative artist is that, since it nourished an agitation of mind, the intensity and duration of which he considered to be the measure of a worthwhile life, it therefore kept alive in him a bright expectancy that marked the style of large portions of the *Life of Samuel Johnson* and of his almost continuous Journal. as well as some of his other writings. Had he not been a Scotsman, the excitement which he experienced in the process of becoming an Englishman and of being accepted into the society of eminent Englishmen of Johnson's circle would not have been possible, and without this excitement his *Life of Samuel Johnson* would hardly have come into being.

It is fairly certain that, before Boswell was sixteen years old, he had already cast his longing eyes in England's direction and had already begun his most sustained and most important literary friendship with an English fellow student at the University of Edinburgh, William Johnson Temple from the nearby village Berwich-on-Tweed, where his father was mayor. Temple earned the Bachelor of Laws degree from Trinity College, Cambridge, and studied law in London, but he later decided on holy orders in the Church of England and held livings first in Devonshire and later in Cornwall. His character of Thomas Gray was used by Johnson in *Lives of the Poets* and by William Mason in his biography of Thomas Gray, he also wrote an essay on clergymen, which was of recognized merit. Aside from producing eleven children from whom two Archbishops of Canterbury descended, probably the most noteworthy fact of Temple's life was his friendship with Boswell, which lasted from University of Edinburgh days until Boswell's death.

In the closing years of his life Boswell referred to Temple as helping to keep alive in him his "love of literature and English manners." Their friendship produced numerous uninhibited letters from Boswell, which are especially valuable for insights into Boswell's personality and for reports in some of them of Boswell's progress in the writing of the biography of Johnson. At one time Boswell suggested to Temple that they publish their letters under the title *Remarks on Various Authors*. This was never done, but many of them have been preserved. Sixty-two years after Boswell's death his share in the correspondence was published separately, his letters having been discovered accidentally in a shop in Boulogne, where they were being used for wrapping paper.

Rough was the English high road that Boswell chose to travel, for many times would he have to stumble over his English friends' prejudices against the Scots and over his own misgivings about them. The chagrin was well founded which he suffered when Johnson told him, during their inauspicious first meeting, that Scotsmen could not help being from Scotland. Boswell had already clearly shown in his Journal that he had an abiding contempt for "Scotch jocularity," familiarity, and crudeness. In his Inviolable Plan, which he drew up as a guide to right conduct when he set forth on his European tour, he ordered himself, "Never indulge the Sarcastical Scotch humour"[1]; and for many years his Journal was to tell of occasions on which he failed or succeeded in this self-command. He found it hard to follow, for while in Edinburgh he would sometimes find himself in sheer self-defense having to assume the "roughness of manners amongst Scotch lawyers." He was so embarrassed by the accent and bearing of his countrymen whenever he encountered them in London that he would shun them. Even Scotland's lord justice clerk, Sir Thomas Miller, when presented to the king, seemed to Boswell "little" in "the great World of London."[2]

The Church of England made Boswell think of heaven and provided some hope that he might ultimately find peaceful refuge there, while his own Church of Scotland filled him with thoughts of hell and offered little encouragement that he would escape its horrors. Despite a brief flirtation with Roman Catholicism and a lifelong attraction to its ritual, Boswell preferred to think of himself as a Church of England man, as he once told Rousseau; and in his Journal he reported attendance at Episcopal services in Edinburgh and London almost as often as at the church of his family. He preferred the solemn ritual of the English church to the "extempore prayers and in short the whole vulgar idea of Presbyterian worship." Once he comforted himself with the inexpedient notion that some day he would officially join the Church of England and even bring one of its chaplains to Auchinleck, his ancestral home, if he should decide to hide himself away in Scotland as the next laird of his father's estate. It was "divinely cheering" to him to think that the English cathedral at Chester was so near Auchinleck.

Boswell's Scottish education was "unlucky," for it was deficient in Greek language and literature; moreover, it left him timid and awkward in the presence of those who were trained in the schools and universities of England. He was at pains to make up for this deficiency by a goodly supply of classical quotations and with a "facility of manners," for which Adam Smith once complimented him.[3] By taking speech lessons, he sought to smooth off the rough edges of his Scottish accent. He had become, in fact, so "retenu" and English in his demeanor that, when he was inducted into the Literary Club, ten years after meeting Johnson, Johnson could say to him, "Sir, I will do you the justice to say that you are the most un-scottified of your countrymen."[4]

But the "descottification" of Boswell was not a simple matter. He never forgot, nor permitted others to forget, that he was "a Scotch gentleman of ancient blood," a claim that was authenticated in the Herald's Office. He was descended from Robert Bruce and, in turn, from James II[5]; his ancestors had been lairds of Auchinleck since 1504, when Thomas Boswell received Auchinleck from James IV in appreciation for military services. Boswell's father, Alexander, holder of the estate on which the ruins of the old castle could still be seen, was a judge of Scotland's High Court and, as such, carried the honorary title of Lord Auchinleck. Boswell's pride in this impressive family position, often reflected in his published and unpublished writings, was, to be sure, a potent force in his life. The ancient castle at Auchinleck and its "romantic rocks and woods" and the family which for centuries had possessed the estate could be destroyed, he declared, only by a fate which no act of his was able to avert. He often projected an image of himself as laird of Auchinleck—dignified, stable, secure in his lordly possessions and many servants and in his respectable niche in Edingurgh's courts. This life his mind told him he should pursue, but it was not the one his heart accepted.

Boswell's feelings about Scotland were, nevertheless, not so unmixed as they often appeared to be. His dilemma was marked by profound complications, as his letters and journals indicate. When Johnson urged Boswell to practice at the English bar, he felt it his patriotic duty to spend his time and substance in Scotland. Further-more, he esteemed the Highland character, in whom he saw "a hardiness of body and a firmness of spirit quite peculiar." On being told by Rosseau that there were "great souls in Spain," he an-swered, "And in the Mountains of Scotland."[6] Despite his love of English ways, he was inclined to regret the loss of Scotland's pecu-liar identity through her union with England. He might have ob-jected to the coarse raillery of his countrymen; but, when he played cards until three o'clock one Sunday morning, he censured himself for having committed an offense against "the notions of decency in Scotland."

His unfavorable opinion of the quality of education in his country did not lessen his pride in the caliber of intellectual fare provided by the group of distinguished persons called in to entertain Johnson when he visited the Scottish capital; and, whenever Johnson and others showed undue contempt for Scotland, he humored them as he would have a child without knowledge or understanding. Al-though Boswell recognized the social and professional advantages of reducing his Scotch accent, he was disgusted whenever he heard a fellow countryman speak the English accent too well. His Tory leanings and his preference for the stately ritual of the English Church failed to diminish his high respect for the democratic func-tioning of the Church of Scotland's governing body. Except when he was temporarily fooled by the Scots poet James Macpherson's forgeries, he showed little enthusiasm for Scots literature; yet among his projected works were a Scotch dictionary, biographies of several of his countrymen, and histories of Edinburgh and of Ayshire, in which was located his native Auchinleck; and he contributed to and helped to edit one of two volumes of poems by "Scotch Gentlemen."

The contour of Boswell's literary career and the tone and content of a number of his writings reflect a soul divided between his love of Scotland's positive virtues and a passion for the social, intellec-tual, and literary excitement offered by London; between a deep respect for sobriety, order, and restraint and impulses that led him from the paths of right living and encouraged wild indulgences in ludicrous fancy. To have Edinburgh and Auchinleck equally with London and soberness equally with passion would have been a devoutly wished-for consummation. When Lord Auchinleck chose Scotland and the law for Boswell, he acquiesced and even tried to make a success of it; but he knew that London would be beckoning. Until near the end of his life he was never able to make a choice that brought him contentment. He rationalized that in human nature there was "a love of permanency, as well as love for variety", and he sought the permanent through marriage and a career in Scotland, but he recklessly pursued variety in London's circle of those whom he often referred to in his Journal as the "gay and ingenious."

It must not be supposed that the company of Johnson and of the men of Johnson's circle was always cause enough to make Boswell's blood tingle. The now famous *London Journal* of 1762-63[7] and other portions of his running Journal tell of his zestful pursuit of an astounding variety of persons and activities. Nor should it be forgotten that at times he merely felt that he had to get away from Scotland's dullness and his father's somber strictures. At any rate, just to be in London was enough. He once wrote to a friend that that life which is not recorded is not valuable, and he proved how little he valued the portion of his life which he spent outside London by the little space he devoted to it in his Journals—such a little, in fact, that one literary historian erroneously stated that Boswell "passed the greater portion of his time in London."[8]

Even before Boswell met Johnson, and just after his visit to London, Boswell could urge his friend Temple to consider his situation as that of a man whose happiness was centered in London, of one "who had at least got there and had begun to taste of its delights— who had got his mind filled with the most gay ideas—getting into the guards, being about the court, enjoying the happiness of the *beau mode* and the company of men of Genius; in short, every thing he could wish—consider this poor fellow hauled away to the town of Edinburgh—obliged to conform to every Scotch custom, . . . his flighty imagination quite cramped."[9] Such was London's attraction for Boswell from the time of his youth to the end of his life that whenever he anticipated a journey to the place or was actually on his way there, he would record his thoughts and feelings with such delight as to suggest that he had to pinch himself to see if he was dreaming. To be in London would never spoil Boswell's dream, except that now and then—especially toward the end of his life —it became a nightmare. He said that one often hears of people who build castles in the air, but he was the first person who ever attempted to live in them. Even after his castle crumbled and its ruins were about his feet, he refused to abandon it.

CHAPTER 2

Apprenticeship

J AMES Boswell was born in Edinburgh in 1740. His father
Alexander Boswell was engaged in the practice of law there and
was later raised to the bench of Scotland's highest court, the Court
of Session. As Lord of Session he took the title of Lord Auchinleck
from the extensive Boswell estate in Ayrshire. James spent many
of his vacations on the estate while attending Mr. Mundell's private
school in Edinburgh and was thus early imbued with a romantic
enthusiasm for his family roots, reaching back for centuries and
connecting with nobility and royalty on both his father's and
mother's sides. Mr. James Mundell introduced him to Addison's
Spectator, which had a lasting influence on his literary and
personal tastes. He was early impressed by Addison's graceful
prose and learned much from him about the fine arts, Latin poetry,
men, and manners. When he entered the University of Edinburgh
at the age of thirteen, the majestic beauty of the Scottish capital
had no less an impact on his mind and spirit than the rugged and
picturesque surroundings of the Ayrshire estate.

While yet only seventeen years old and a student at the university,
Boswell was hard at work trying to think and act like a man of
letters, but he knew that he was doomed to pursue the law as a
profession or suffer the wrath of his father. He had already
cultivated the acquaintance of David Hume, the Scots philosopher,
whom he admired for his learning and collection of books; and he
had conversed with him about "genius, fine language and
improving style."[1] He found encouragement in the friendship and
patronage of Sir David Dalrymple, distinguished Scots lawyer and
antiquarian, and the colorful and adventurous Scotsman and
seventh Lord Somerville, whose home near Edinburgh was a
rallying point for sundry personalities of the theatrical and
literary world. A man of ancient family, Somerville, distinguished
himself at court and enjoyed the distinction of being assigned
private apartments in one of the royal palaces. Naturally, the

young Boswell was flattered by the solicitous attention of a man
of such high rank, who, furthermore, had numbered Alexander
Pope among his close acquaintances. Somerville encouraged Boswell in his literary pursuits and excited in him restless anticipation
of London. Before arriving at the age of eighteen, Boswell had
already tried his hand at prose essays and poems, and his letters
to Temple were stocked with observations about men and books.

I The Lure of Literary Fame—and London

Boswell's first literary effort extant was the poem "An Evening
Walk in the Abbey-Church of Holyrood-house," which appeared in
the Scots Magazine for August, 1758.[2] Ordinary as it is, it shows
a competence in the handling of perfectly regular end-stopped
blank verse; and it conceivably impressed some of his contemporaries as a rather successful expression of one of the currently
fashionable moods:

> Such is the present time, now sober Eve,
> Has drawn her Sable curtain o're the earth
> And hush'd the busy world to soft repose.
> Come then, my Soul, compose each faculty,
> And bid thy restless passions be at peace.
> Here's room for sacred, solemn meditation,
> Pleasing employment of the serious mind.

Within a few weeks the Scots Magazine was to carry two more of
his poems, one a mere epigram occasioned by the death of the
comedian Theophilus Cibber and the other a humorous poem in
doggerel on the marriage of "a beautiful lady" to "a coarse hulk
of a Gentleman." In his brief Memoirs, which appeared in the
European Magazine four years before his death, Boswell wrote that
at this early period of his life he had published some prose essays.
One of them, because of its similarity in content and mood to "An
Evening Walk," is almost certainly "A Contemplative Walk at
Moffat, on a Summer-night."[3]

Boswell's eagerness for a literary career and for the society of wits
is suggested in the little that we know of his brief sojourn in the
University of Glasgow, for he foresook Edinburgh in the fall of
1759 as he was entering his nineteenth year. He matriculated at
Glasgow expressly to study civil law; but it must have occupied
only a small share of his attention, for we find him attending

Adam Smith's lectures in philosophy and belles lettres, wangling a dedication to himself of an inferior play by an Irish actor, Francis Gentleman, entitled *Oroonoka*, and packing up for London in the spring of 1760, before completion of the term.[4] Prior to leaving Edinburgh, Boswell had already shown an interest in the theater by producing a notoriously unsuccessful comedy by Lady Houston, a distant relative; and, while in Glasgow, he was perhaps often in the company of actors and actresses since an unfounded rumor connected his precipitate departure from Scotland with one of them.[5] The circumstances of his leaving for London and of his embracing the Roman Catholic faith, which expediency forced him to abandon as quickly as he had accepted it, are somewhat hazy but need not detain us here. The fact is that he acquired "from reading and conversation an almost enthusiastic notion of the felicity of London," as he wrote in his Journal, and he wished no longer to delay his visit there.

Boswell did not leave a running account of this London sojourn of three months as he was to do of the next trip two years later. We must, then, rely upon scattered accounts in letters, incidental comments in the Journals, and a few other items that have come to light since discovery of the Boswell papers. Had he written a journal of this jaunt, it would no doubt have had its exciting moments, but it might have lacked the aplomb and zest that mark his account of the later visit when he was more experienced in finding his way about.

No sooner had he reached the capital than he plunged into enjoyment of its seamy aspects under the tutelage of Samuel Derrick, an author of no reputation whom he later despised and shunned. Through Derrick, he met the gadabouts and lesser literati. But it was to the earl of Eglinton, a fellow Scotsman from Ayrshire then living in London, that he was indebted for his introduction to the socially and intellectually prominent. Through Eglinton's good graces he met and breakfasted with John Home, the then very widely known dramatist whose *Seige of Acquila* had just been produced and who as secretary to Lord Bute, the prime minister, enjoyed the patronage of the royal family; the novelist Laurence Sterne, who during these weeks was in London basking in the dizzy heights of his suddenly won fame; and no less a personage than his royal highness the duke of York, a gentleman not at all disdainful of the more boisterous pleasures of the *beau*

monde. During this first stay in London Boswell found himself
also in the company of David Garrick, the actor, and of James
Dodsley, the younger member of the Dodsley book firm. It may be
that this early he hoped to form the acquaintance of Samuel
Johnson, but we know of no efforts on his part to do so; and he was
not yet to be introduced to the writer Horace Walpole, even though
he had the opportunity, for he felt that Walpole moved "in rather
too high a sphere for your Humble servant, whose company would
of consequence be rather burthensome to him."[6]

That Boswell and Sterne hobnobbed on several occasions has
been convincingly indicated by Professor Pottle, who attributes
to Boswell two items relating to Sterne.[7] The first of these is
"An Original Letter, from a Gentleman of Scotland to the Earl
of °°° in London," which appeared in the *Scots Magazine.*[8] The
writer inquired about Sterne, whom, he said, was the best companion he ever knew. The other item, "Epistle to Sterne," is one of
several poems contained in a manuscript found in the Bodleian. In
competent doggerel the author describes some of Sterne's
idiosyncracies and reminiscences about their good times together.
Boswell may have written Sterne once after his return to Scotland,
but their paths never crossed again before the latter's death five
years after the London visit.

Not all aspects of Sterne's influence on Boswell have hitherto
been noticed; immediate and crazy, it was fortunately brief. It
showed itself first in his *The Cub at New-Market*, written in
1760, though not published until 1762. In the Preface, which outdid
Sterne in its jocular absurdities, Boswell informed his readers that
he published the poem because of its merit and that he wished to
furnish friends with copies of it. Futhermore, it had been approved
by those "whose taste it would be the highest arrogance in me to
call in question." The next item to come from Boswell's pen
(published earlier but written later than *The Cub*) was *Observations, Good or Bad, Stupid or Clever, Serious or Jocular, on
Squire Foote's Dramatic Entertainment, entitled, The Minor By a
Genius* (1760). The title, the prefatory imaginary conversation
between the Genius and the Parson, and the beginning and ending
of the essay are all poor imitations of Sterne.

But Boswell was soon to become disenchanted with his idol. He
wrote in his Journal that the extravagance of *Tristram Shandy* was
tiring: "We have just a succession of surprise, surprise, surprise."[9]

He later objected to Sterne's "levity" and "much contaminating extravagance of effusion";[10] and he held that imitations adopt not the virtues but the faults of celebrated writers—that many, for instance, had made themselves ridiculous by imitating Sterne's "sudden sallies of fancy and unconnected breakes of sentiment."[11] He disapproved, in fact, of his own imitation of Sterne in the *Observations*, which, because of its manner and its ideas, he later judged as "an idle performance, and written inconsiderately."[12]

The *Observations*, Boswell's first separate publication, is not a dramatic criticism of Foote's *The Minor* but a comment on a phase of it relating to the Methodist revival, which, according to Leslie Stephen,[13] was "in many respects by far the most important phenomenon of the century." After some Shandean clowning, Boswell began the serious part of the booklet by distinguishing between what he considered the real intention of the play, which concerned the efforts of Sir William Wealthy to reclaim his young blade George (the Minor), and what can easily be mistaken for the real intention: the delineation of "the character in it that has made the most noise, the old Covent Garden bawd Mrs. Cole, 'a zealous devotee' of Methodism." He fully approved of Foote's condemnation of the Methodists for their "new birth and a set of supernatural feelings, in the place of regular and virtuous conduct"; their "miraculous conversion"; and "distempered reveries and uncouth cant"—all of which, he stated, are supported by the "ignorant, unstable and easily deluded rabble who are carried away by every wind of doctrine."

We do not know of Boswell's ever again writing or speaking with such contempt of the Methodists; and, when he later condemned his own absurd style in the *Observations*, he also expressed regret for his approval of the ideas in Foote's play, which were, upon sober consideration, "profane and illiberal."[14] He came to know what students of the period now understand, and that is that, while the evangelical movement, like many movements, had its aberrations, they were, as is true of all aberrations, untypical. No doubt Boswell was well acquainted with the ridiculous behavior of certain religious enthusiasts, including some Methodists; but he nevertheless wished to "do justice to those whom it is the fashion to ridicule without knowledge of their tenets."[15] As a matter of fact, he later became impressed with the earnestness of Wesley's followers and with the "methodical attention to devout exercises" that distinguished those students at Oxford University who founded Methodism in 1729. And he observed that Samuel Johnson, his moral and religious conselor for many years, had shown similar tendencies in his *Prayers and Meditations*. The contrast between Boswell's later attitude toward the most significant religious movement of his time and his youthful outburst of smart-alecky vituperation in the *Observations* is rather remarkable, for he seldom changed his attitudes and opinions. As we find him in the 1790's, so had he been, for the most part, in the 1760's.

His next work to enjoy separate publication was an adolescent trick that bespoke a craving for literary recognition: *An Elegy on the Death of an Amiable Young Lady with An Epistle from Menalcas to Lycidas, to which are prefixed Three Critical Recommendatory Letters* (1761). This work was an anonymous publication of two of his poems along with discussions of them in the form of letters by, respectively, himself and two literary cronies who were in on the hoax—Andrew Erskine and George Dempster. Erskine was the younger son of the fifth earl of Kellie, a Scottish colonel in the Jacobite army during the Rebellion of 1745. His father became impoverished because of the failure of the rebellion, contributing thereby to the instability of Andrew. He had met Boswell earlier at Fort George; and, at the time of Boswell's second trip to London in 1763, he was in the British army on half pay. Like Boswell, of whom he never was a close friend, he was a rather prolific versifier and a hypochondriac, and therefore just the kind of literary companion Boswell needed at this time. Dempster, the third collaborator in this juvenile enterprise, was a Scotsman who had inherited a comfortable fortune. He attended the University of St. Andrews, and he was later a member of the Faculty of Advocates, a member of Parliament, and secretary of the Scottish Order of the Thistle. He wrote several papers for the Royal Society of Edinburgh, but he never distinguished himself as a writer. During Boswell's visits to London, Dempster and Erskine were often in his company.

The advertisement to *An Elegy* explained that these obliging gentlemen, not ashamed of encouraging genius, permitted publication of their opinions; for they regarded them as "the warm overflowings of souls susceptible of the ravishing beauties of geniune poetry." The "dizzy summit" of the second line in the quatrain which follows was effusively recommended by the first encourager of genius, none other than Boswell himself:

> Let me, whose humbler muse hath ne'er aspired
> To such majestic, such exalting strains
> By elegiac song be now inspired
> And mourn a virgin snatched from these plains.

His third publication was also his third literary prank in 1761. Signing "A Gentleman from Scotland," to his *Ode to Tragedy*, he dedicated it to James Boswell, a man of "extensive erudition" for whom the productions of the tragic muse were as palatable as "the most brilliant sallies of sportive Fancy." In the *Observation* he had indicated exposure to contemporary speculations on the sublime, and in the *Ode to Tragedy* he reflected literary doctrine and method that rendered the third quarter of the eighteenth century a period of transition from neoclassical to romantic moods and emphases. While couching his thoughts in the stilted phraseology of much of the poetry of his time and while uttering conventional tribute to the buskined stage of ancient Greece, he recognized the claims of genius as against the authority of mechanical rules of art. He praised Shakespeare for his "Genius unbounded as the sky" and for his lively depiction of "witches and all the magic train," and he attacked the "tasteless critics" who complained that the Bard had broken "all rules of art." The practice of Shakespeare was adduced in support of eighteenth-century poets and critics who favored the heart as a guide to right conduct: "To the kind heart alone thou dost appeal,/ And bidst the ingenuous there conviction feel."

So far Boswell has focussed his efforts principally on poetry, and they were mainly wistful dilly-dallying. Hardly more can be said for his contributions to the second volume of *A Collection of Original Poems by Scotch Gentlemen* (1762), for which he and one of his collaborators in the publication of the *Elegy*, Andrew Erskine, did most of the editorial hackwork and contributed enough poems together to constitute 95 out of the 232 pages of the book. Other writers of the collection, which is now one of the rarest of the Boswell items extant, were George Dempster, previously mentioned as the author of one of the recommendatory letters for the *Elegy*; James Macpherson; John Home; John Ogilvie; and about twenty others hardly heard of since 1762. Several of Boswell's poems in the book had already found their way to the *Scots Magazine*, as had "An Evening Walk," which also appears in this volume. It is not worse than other pieces in the collection, and it is better than most of his later attempts.

The majority of Boswell's verses in *Original Poems* are brief epigrams, written chiefly in light and humorous vein. They celebrate
the experience of being jilted by Kitty, a lady lulled asleep by the
essay of a mutual friend, an acquaintance taking to his heels in a
fight, an ass striving to pass for what he is not, and the like. Several
are not wholly ineffective; yet they are hardly worthy of inclusion in
a book labeled "poetry." When, for instance, a good bishop advised
British Nell to refrain from writing poetry since poetesses and light-
heads were one and the same thing, she agreed that heavy heads
could never succeed in writing verses; but she thought the Right
Reverend gentleman might spare his sage maxims: "Cork becomes
us much better than lead becomes you." Boswell's apostrophe to
currant jelly, in the frivolous mood of many of the poems by other
contributors, suggests the extremes to which some writers would go
in departing from what prescriptive critics considered to be the
proper bounds of the material and treatment of poetry:

> O what a rapture did my palate feel!
> How didst thou, jelly, delicately steal,
> With pleasing power, through all my thrilling frame,
> And make me vow to consecrate thy name.

As devoid of merit as these verses are, they are superior to the
serious epigrams and other serious short poems. In the epigraph on
the Reverend John Campbell (alongside the apostrophe to currant
jelly), for instance, the reader is proffered the shockingly banal
advice to "Remember that the minutes quickly fly,/And that the
time will come when you must die." Boswell's "Ode on the Death
of Marshal Keith" is in the manner of contemporary Pindaric imitations. The invocation could easily be mistaken for a parody of the
genre:

> Melpomene, divine, Saturnian maid!
>   Propitious to my numbers lend thine aid;
>   my bosom fire:
> O while I raise the plaintive song,
> Descend from the celestial throng,
>   And guide the lyre.

II   *The Quest Renewed*

With the venture of *Original Poems* out of the way, Boswell eagerly anticipated another trip to London. He had enjoyed his first visit and had even fraternized with a famous writer and with royalty; but now he wanted to obtain a commission in the Guards and to establish himself in the literary and social life of the city. During his second sojourn, recounted fully in his *London Journal* of 1762-63 and in the *Life of Samuel Johnson,* he resumed his relations with Eglinton and other socially prominent persons and eventually managed an introduction to Samuel Johnson himself, who made no profound change in Boswell but served as a counselor and spiritual guide and stimulated him in the pursuit of goals to which he had already dedicated his life.

Erskine and Dempster, with whom Boswell had previously collaborated in the publication of juvenilia, were now in London; and the renewal of his associations with them led to his next writing venture. These three seekers of notoriety, hearing that David Mallet's tragedy *Elvira* was opening on the night of January 19, 1763, planned to disrupt the performance with loud boisterousness. They detested the author because he had changed his name from typical Scottish Malloch and for other reasons. Failing to win enough of the audience to follow through with their wrecking plans, they gave it up as a lost cause. Not to be fully outdone, however, they published their sentiments in *Critical Strictures on the New Tragedy of Elvira written by David Malloch* (1763), the first draft of which was so ruthless in its attacks on the author and the play that Flexney, the bookseller, sent it back for revision. The published second draft is scathing enough, but Boswell's contribution seems to be meager. The light, clever touch was not his but that of one or both of the other authors, who gave devastating expression to the pooled criticism leveled against the tragedy's burlesque quality and to what they deemed false depiction of human nature and its improprieties. They charged that what Malloch stole outright from the owners was so insignificant that he should be brought in "guilty of Petty Larceny."

Although Boswell was not to consider himself an author until the issuance of his book on Corsica, he had a hand in six publications before his twenty-sixth birthday. Two were commentaries on plays, two were poems, one was a combination of poetry and criticism, and one a collection of poems to which he and Erskine were the principal contributors. Boswell was eventually to acknowledge authorship of each, but not until the appearance of *Letters between*

The Honourable Andrew Erskine, and James Boswell, Esq. (1763) was his name seen on a title page. The fourth and last collaboration between Boswell and Erskine, this project was begun during the interim between Boswell's first two visits to London; and the literary interests and activities described in the pages of the book belong to that period, although final plans for publication did not materialize until Boswell and Erskine continued their association in London in 1762 and 1763.

With this volume of letters Boswell and his collaborator imagined that they were launching with full tackle into the literary sea. The streamers were painted all around, announcing in bright colors the destination of the ship's inexperienced but adventurous cocaptains. The selfconsicous straining after witty effects in many of the letters and the obvious determination to sound as literary as possible should not be allowed to obscure the actual interests of the two correspondents and what the letters, which did pass through the mails, revealed of their activities at the time. Professor C. B. Tinker perhaps too readily dismissed them as mere trifles and excluded those written by Boswell from his valuable edition of Boswell's letters.[16] It is doubtful whether either of the correspondents took the letters very seriously, or themselves for that matter. To be sure, they desired public notice; but, at the same time, they thought the letters might bring some amusement to a small but definite public, composed principally of their relatives, friends, and acquaintances in Edinburgh and London.

The book's emphasis is clearly literary, not social. In the first letter Boswell inquired about a certain "elegant Lady A," but not until the eighteenth do we find the first mention of a social event—the splendid ball at the Royal Palace Holyroodhouse on the Queen's birthday. Several of the letters are about Macpherson's recently published *Fingal*, which was causing a sensation in London's reading circles. Boswell assured Erskine that *Fingal* would make him feel that he had a soul. (Later he discarded this good opinion of the poem and became convinced that it was a hoax.) Suspense was rather cleverly achieved by the exchange of letters describing Erskine's reaction to reading the *Ode to Tragedy* and his eagerness to know the identity of its author, the "Gentleman from Scotland," who had dedicated it to Boswell; and Boswell at last revealed his own authorship of the poem. There was much talk of the forthcoming *Original Poems* and of the dinner to which Donaldson, its publisher, invited Boswell, "the only author in the company." The correspondents sometimes discussed examples of their own writing, which they not infrequently enclosed for criticism; and they often exchanged views about the works of other writers, mainly contemporary and recent ones.

We see in one of the letters an early indication of Boswell's negative response to his century's recurrent vogue of rural blessedness and of his thoroughly Augustan tastes. He had spent an entire forenoon wandering through Auchinleck, which he thought was "the sweetest place in the world"; but he failed to follow through with his description of that place, as we are led to believe he was about to do. Instead, he revealed what was actually on his mind: the world of affairs. He was looking forward to

The brillant scenes of happiness which I shall enjoy as an officer in the guards, . . . the grandeur of a court, . . . many fine jaunts to the noble seats of dukes, lords, and members of parliament, . . . the perfect knowledge which I shall acquire of men and manners, of the intimacies which I shall have the honour to form with the learned and ingenious in every science, and of amusing literary anecodotes which I shall pick up. I am thinking of making the tour of Europe, and feasting on the delicious prospects of Italy and France; of feeling all the transport of a bard at Rome, and writing noble poems on the banks of the Tiber.

Boswell never obtained his commission in the Guards, and he never wrote noble poems; but he achieved many of the other desires expressed here—and, each time he did, he reacted with the naïve delight of a child. Twenty-eight years later, as he was describing in his Journal a magnificent gathering which he enjoyed at Lord Palmerston's, he recalled the youthful expectancy of that letter: "I was actually in one of the scenes which I figure in a letter to the Hon. A. Erskine.[17]

In August, 1763, four months following publication of the Boswell-Erskine correspondence, Boswell, a young man of twenty-three, left Harwich for a three-year sojourn on the Continent; and his new friend Samuel Johnson waved good-by until the ship was out of sight. Boswell was not to publish another book for four years, if we except his thesis on legacies of household furniture, *Disputatio Juridica* (1766), which he submitted to the University of Edinburgh and which he had privately printed. And only rarely during this time did he send any of his scribblings to periodicals. He was too busy storing up experiences, making literary contacts, and "just educating for a Periodical Writer."[18]

Brief mention of his experiences in Europe must suffice, but copious accounts of them are available in *The Private Papers of James Boswell* and in three of the volumes of the Yale Editions of these papers.[19] Boswell remained in Utrecht a few months, but much of his time during the three years was spent in the pursuit of social pleasures and cultural stimulation. Meanwhile, he did not waver in his determination to cut a figure in the world of letters; and he never lost an opportunity to meet the people who, he thought, could further his literary interests. In Ferney, Switzerland, he enjoyed the hospitality of Voltaire, to whom he showed some of his poems; he could boast of more than a passing acquaintance with Rousseau, whom he visited in Motiers, Switzerland; he called on Thomas Gray and John Wilkes in Italy; and, to the already impressive number of his durable friendships, he added that of the famous General Paoli in Corsica.

When Boswell returned to London, Johnson, impressed with what Boswell had related to him of his experiences, said, "Now you have five and twenty years, and you have employed 'em well . . . though you may know no science so well as to be able to teach it, and no profession as well as to be able to follow it, yet your general mass of knowledge of books and men renders you very capable to study any science or follow any profession."[20]

III   *The Douglas Miscellany*

Boswell undoubtedly felt a new confidence when he returned from the Continent. He quickly came to grips with his law duties in Edinburgh, and he soon began extensive campaigning for two famous causes that occasioned the most concentrated journalistic activity of his whole career and the publication of six separate items. One of these was the case of Archibald Douglas, the putative heir to extensive holdings of an old Scottish family, whose inheritance was being contested in the courts. When Archibald Stuart, who had not yet reached his majority, was named heir to the immense estates of the duke of Douglas, he was opposed by the family of the duke of Hamilton, who was also not yet of age, on the grounds that Archibald was not the nephew of the duke of Douglas, as it was claimed he was, but had been abducted from his indigent French father by the duke's sister and her husband in order to inherit the Douglas estates by trickery. Furthermore, the Hamiltons argued legal claim to the property. Archibald's mother, Lady Jane Douglas, had gone to France and married in secret because her brother the duke disapproved of her poor but genteel husband, Colonel John Stuart. To complicate additionally the situation, the births of Archibald and a twin brother who died at the age of four took place in a lodging house in Paris under guarded circumstances that were difficult to verify on demand.

Counsel for the duke of Hamilton sought to prove that the two boys were the children of a French glass manufacturer and a rope-dancer. Interested in the case as a lawyer, a writer, and a fervent believer in the prerogatives of ancient family status, Boswell served as one of the counsels for Douglas in the Scottish Court of Session; but we do not find him appearing for Douglas before the House of Lords, to which the case had been appealed after Douglas lost the decision in the Edinburgh court.[21] The personal aspect of Boswell's interest in the outcome of the dispute can be seen in a letter that he wrote to Sir Alexander Dick: "I am for the descent of an ancient family, who after an obscurity of several generations, lays claims to the estate of his forefathers. You know my old feudal soul and how a cause of this kind must interest me."[22]

Boswell's writings on the Douglas case were brought forward after the close of the Edinburgh phase of the contest; and it was to them that, with some justification, he attributed the final victory in the House of Lords. "With a labor of which few are capable," Boswell recorded in his *Memoirs*[23] several years later, he had "compressed the substance of the immense volumes of proofs and arguments" in the Court of Session into a pamphlet entitled *The Essence of the Douglas Cause* (1767). The advertisement and a few introductory remarks comprise the burden of Boswell's written contribution, but the *Essence*, marked by restrained, thorough, and objective application, is a product of that industry and sense of dedication for which Boswell now and then demonstrated a strong aptitude. The advertisement in eighteenth-century books was generally a brief statement, which, like the modern preface, was a part of the front matter. More often than not, it carried chatty author-to-reader comments on the nature of the work and its significance, as well as acknowledgments of indebtedness to various persons for special assistance. The advertisement in question here echoed Boswell's continuing interest in ancient family prerogatives and a very special and personal concern for the inviolability of the law of birthright; for his father, displeased with his irregular habits and his London literary ambitions, had threatened more than once to cut him off from his inheritance.

Boswell's next work, *Dorando, A Spanish Tale* (1767), was an allegorical representation of the main facts of the Douglas story. In this fifty-page romance somewhat after the manner of Walpole's *The Castle of Otranto*, Don Carlos, prince of Dorando, is meant for the duke of Douglas. He had no brothers, but he did have an honorable, educated, and pious sister, the Princess Maria (Lady Jane Douglas), who for many years discouraged the attentions of suitors but in her forty-seventh year accepted the hand of the Cavalier Don Spiritoso and went to France to marry him in secret. The prince, whose estate was near Dorando and who was intent upon securing succession to the Dorando estate through trickery, had prejudiced Carlos against Don Spiritoso. While in France, Maria gave birth to twins; but Arvidoso convinced Carlos that she had only counterfeited the births. Shortly after her return to Spain, where she was denied admittance to the family castle, she and her younger son died, leaving only Ferdinand, the real heir to Dorando. Before his death, Carlos became aware of his errors, dissolved Arvidoso's claims to the Dorando estate, and assigned it to Don Ferdinand. No sooner had Carlos died than Ferdinand's enemies, the Arvidosos, hoping to get possession of the Dorando estate, instituted a process against Ferdinand.

Both families sent great lawyers to France for the case, and volumes of evidence were produced on both sides. Needless to say, the House of Dorando was victorious. The chief justice is Boswell, the young Scots advocate and the proud son of a feudal family who attacks the intention of the process "to stigmatize with infamy a princess of the noblest blood in Europe." Boswell's points in support of the Douglases are made with expert clarity, and his excellently subdued style, though deficient in local color, is suggestive of competence in a genre in which he might have had some success had he put his mind to it.

The book that perhaps had the most powerful effect was *Letters of the Right Honourable Lady Jane Douglas* (1767), in which the editors, of whom Boswell was only one, collected and selected their material so as to highlight Lady Jane's pathetic situation and the goodness of her character. Subjoined to these letters were the deathbed confessions of Lady Jane; Sir John Stuart, her husband; and their attendant, Mrs. Helen Hunt. *The Douglas Cause,* Boswell's poem published in 1767 as a broadside, also reveals his Tory sympathies. He warned that

> Should noble Douglas lose his cause
>   Foes may 'gainst all our Families dance in,
> And ev'ry egg-shell of a plea
> Become a boat to sail to France in.

Regarding his endeavors in support of Archibald Douglas, Boswell explained that he "took care to keep the newspapers and other publications incessantly warm with various writings, both in prose and verse, all tending to touch the heart and rouse the parental and sympathetic feelings."[24] These periodical items have too scant a literary value to dwell upon, but they are significant as early indications of that indefatigable industry which was characteristic of Johnson's biographer when he had attached himself to a cause. They include extracts in five installments of a number of publications relating to the case,[25] letters between Boswell and the Honorable Miss Primrose about a dispute between themselves regarding the case,[26] and correspondence that had taken place between Lady Jane and a Mr. Pelham in which the latter announced success in his attempts to enlist financial help from the king for relief of Lady Jane's destitute condition.[27]

Corsican independence was the other cause for which Boswell worked diligently and energetically with his pen. His journalistic activities in its behalf (and, it would seem, in his own behalf) and his first important book, which was a product of it, merit consideration.

CHAPTER 3

Corsica and Literary Recognition

I N Boswell's one-man campaign to rouse the sympathy of fellow Britons for the Corsicans' valiant struggle for independence from Genoa, Boswell kept the London and Edinburgh periodicals constantly supplied with various writings, as he had done in connection with the Douglas case. The background of this volley of miscellaneous items constitutes the most romantic chapter of his venturesome life. "As long as I can remember anything," he wrote, "I have heard of 'the Malcontents of Corsica with Paoli at their head.' "[1] He had also read Rousseau's impressive tribute to the brave Corsicans in *The Social Contract*: "There is still one country in Europe capable of legislation—the island of Corsica. The courage and determination with which its brave people have recovered and defended their liberty deserves that some wise men teach it how it may be preserved. I have a premonition that this tiny island may one day astonish Europe."[2]

Having thus spoken favorably of Corsica as a nation with strong instincts for political and social liberty, Rousseau was asked by one of the Corsican leaders to assist in the preparation of a constitution. When Boswell saw Rousseau in Switzerland, he told him of his desire to go to Corsica, and he wrote to him from Rome asking for a letter of introduction to General Pascal Paoli. The colorful general had for a decade distinguished himself by intelligent and heroic leadership; and by 1765, the year of Boswell's visit, he had driven the Genoese to the shores while France was occupying parts of the island for defensive purposes.

I   The Corsica Miscellany

Boswell released a barrage of Corsican items to the British newspapers before and after his return to England from the Continent. His aim was to engage the active support of the British people for the Corsicans, who had not yet capitulated to the Genoese, and, meanwhile, to attract public attention to himself as he conducted what was in actuality a publicity campaign for his forthcoming book about Corsica. Some of the reports submitted to the periodicals were true accounts; others are now known to be sheer inventions, for he so informed posterity in his own marked file of the *London Chronicle*, where many of the entries first appeared before being reprinted by various other periodicals.[3]

The first of these items was an invention of Boswell's in the form of a letter from Rome dated December 5, 1765. It stated that a report was being circulated to the effect that the British government was sending an ambassador to Corsica and that it was a certain fact that a British subject, Mr. Boswell, a Scots gentleman, had gone as far as a hundred miles into the country and had been received by Paoli "with every distinction." Despite Mr. Boswell's saying he went there for curiosity, the letter continued, the popiticians thought there were "more important reasons." A few days later, as if the curiosity of his countrymen were not already sufficiently awakened, there appeared an article under the apparently authentic heading "Foreign Intelligence," reporting a rumor that perhaps Mr. Boswell's mission had to do with establishing the young pretender to the British throne as king of Corsica.

Other articles and letters—some signed, others not—chided the freedom-loving British for indifference to spirited little Corsica that had been struggling against oppression for thirty years; invented a dashing Corsican courier of profound learning who was visiting at The Hague; stated the sentiments of an English merchant about Corsica's struggles and about the obligations of his countrymen; solicited funds for the cause; and gave accounts of the Corsican occupation of the neighboring island of Capraya. Meanwhile, Boswell was submitting to the newspapers articles and letters of an informative nature to which he affixed his signature; and he was no doubt responsible for the following entry establishing himself as the authority on Corsican affairs: "As many of our readers are desirous of being informed whether they may depend on the authenticity of our Corsican news, we are allowed to inform them, that whatever appears in *The London Chronicle* under the article of Corsican Gazette, or Corsican Intelligence, is communicated to us by Mr. Boswell, to whom regular information is transmitted by General Paoli; and that the above gentleman has just favored us with General Paoli's manifesto, addressed to the People of Corsica."[4]

Thus, by a prolonged championship of the Corsicans, conducted in person and through the press, Boswell cleverly prepared for the appearance in February, 1768, of his first book of unquestionable literary value: *An Account of Corsica, the Journal of a Tour to That Island, and Memoirs of Pascal Paoli*. This book brought the kind of recognition he craved. In the Preface to the first edition, he wrote with disarming frankness that he wanted to be known as an author; for he valued literary fame above all other possessions. In the Preface to the third edition, published in 1769, he could joyfully report, "I have obtained my desire."

The book is made up of two separate and distinct works: the *Account* and *The Journal of a Tour to Corsica.* "Memoirs of Paoli," a part of the *Tour*, is mainly a record of Boswell's interviews with Paoli. The *Account*, coming first and extending to 258 pages, is not the part that brought fame to its author. It was, in fact, the *Tour,* which is less than half the size of the *Account*, and which has been published and translated into other languages more often during and since Boswell's time.[5] It is not difficult to understand the advantage of the *Tour* over the *Account*: it presents the author's unique and uncommonly interesting experiences, whereas the latter is made up almost exclusively of material painstakingly gathered from books and other published items.

With a bounce that Boswell had already established as rather typically Boswellian, he stated in his Preface to the *Account* that this book had been expected for some time and that he had been encouraged by the public's couriosity. Everywhere he went, he continued, people asked him about the island and its natives. Furthermore, Paoli, knowing of his acquaintance with the country, its inhabitants, and its constitution, was pleased to have him write about Corsica. He, the author, was justifiably proud of his being the only Briton to have gone into its interior. He ended his introductory remarks with a salute to liberty and with a rousing tribute to the Corsicans' patriotic virtue and noble pursuit of freedom, of which his book would serve to communicate.

II   The Account of Corsica

The first part of the *Account* includes a geographical and physical description of Corsica. Asserting that Pliny's, and not Seneca's, geographical particulars were accurate, Boswell described the island's exact location and its summer and winter climate and men-

tioned its abundance of good harbors. He enlivened his collection
of factual materials with bits of curious information: there remained standing many ancient towers, especially in the north, that
had been built three or four hundred years earlier to defend the
inhabitants against the Turks and other pirates; the Romans had
had two colonies on the island but, excepting a few "pretty good"
engravings on stones, hardly any other traces of Roman grandeur
remained; low marshy grounds in some sections of the country
were so conducive to sickness that not many people could bear to
live there; garrisons stationed in such territory, consequently, had
to be changed each month.

Boswell then demonstrated that, for other reasons, large portions
of this wild, bleak island were uninhabitable. It consisted mainly
of woods to which the peasants resorted in order to feed cattle and
gather chestnuts. Hardly a farm house was to be seen; for most
Corsicans preferred the safety and social life of the villages, which
were often built at the top of high hills or mountains. The large
and beautiful rivers were generally unnavigable; for, after heavy
rains, torrents tumbled from the mountains bringing fragments
of rocks large enough to dash to pieces any boats that might be
passing at the time.

What the island yielded in foods and provisions could hardly
serve to counteract the negative appeal that it would have had for
Boswell's British and continental contemporaries. Its hot and cold
mineral springs, to be sure, were said to furnish cures for distempers;
much wine was produced from its abundant supply of grapes and
honey from its many bees; its rivers and sea coasts abounded in good
fish; and poisonous animals were not to be found (even scorpions
and spiders carried no venom). But pastures were so scarce that cows
produced little milk, and the few sheep that were not destroyed by
large and ravenous foxes yielded only coarse, hairy wool. The farm
instruments were crude, and agriculture was poorly developed.
Furthermore, the men were lazy; the women, consequently, did
most of the drudgery.

As might be expected, Boswell's account of this country of many
mountains and isolated villages took due notice of the arts and
appurtenances of civilization which flourished in a few towns,
mainly under the influence and support of the French. Bastia, the
largest of them, had a castle, a cathedral, an elegant Jesuit church
and college, as well as Franciscan and Capuchin convents. Ajaccio,

whose inhabitants were the most genteel people on the island, had handsome streets, beautiful walks, and a citadel and palace for the Genoese governor. The university in Corte was not without distinction. Corte served as capital under Paoli, and his castle stood upon a rock perpendicular on all sides. It was almost impregnable, since the winding passage leading up to it admitted only two persons abreast.

After describing the appearance of the country and some of the means by which the natives extracted their living from the land, Boswell touched upon different aspects of Corsica's history, particularly upon the political changes that it had undergone through the centuries. Herodotus, he wrote, gave us our earliest account of Corsica; and the Phoenicians were its first inhabitants. Boswell, rejecting the taste of his age for demonstrable proof in historical matters, preferred to speculate about the "dark and fabulous" subject of Corsica's origin; and he would not discount the probability that Cadmus, a Phoenician in search of Europe, fell upon the island. The first certain knowledge of the Corsicans was that they were under the rule of the Carthaginians and then of the Romans about the middle of the fifth century, when they refused, as at the time of Boswell's visit, to bear subjection patiently.

Eventually the Corsicans were conquered by the Goths, the Saracens, and the popes. From the early fourteenth to the eighteenth centuries, the power shifted several times between the Genoese and the French. When the young Pascal Paoli, born in Corsica but educated in Naples, returned to Corsica in 1755, it was in the hands of the Genoese; but he soon drove them to the remote corners of the island. Boswell brought his survey up to date as he pointed out that, when Paoli had almost completely freed every part of the island from the Genoese, a treaty was concluded between France and Genoa in which the French agreed to send batallions of troops, in 1764, to garrison the fortified towns in Corsica.

Boswell ended his documentary work on Corsica with an exposition of the Corsicans' internal political situation. Along with a fierce love of a national freedom and the right to determine their own national destiny, he pointed out, went an ingrained sense of political democracy that had appeared centuries ahead of its time. Highly loyal Roman Catholics, the Corsicans were nevertheless opposed to any interference in the national government on the part of the church. Paoli's skill as a head of state is indicated in the proper

balance which he maintained between church and state and between peasants and feudal lords, or "Signers," who, afraid of for-
feiting their domains, had hesitated to join the peasants against
the Genoese. When these lords applied to Paoli for the restitution
of their ancient rights, he was careful not to offend the peasants,
who were unwilling to exchange subjugation under the Genoese for
subjugation under the feudal lords. He was also careful not to offend
the lords and thus disturb the smooth cooperation of the government. He solved the problem by leaving the lords with only minor
powers—to determine causes, for instance, but not to sentence.
Boswell, who enjoyed thoughts of his feudal descent, wrote this
phase of his treatise in tones suggesting deep pleasure that the hereditary feudal jurisdiction of the lords had been moderated but
not destroyed.

Despite his excursion into "the dark backward and abysm of
time," as he employed legend and myth to explain who the original
inhabitants were, the *Account* nevertheless has practical value as
a clearly written and factual description of the geography and the
topography of the country and as a discussion of its conditions in
the eighteenth century. For these reasons, it is still listed in bibliographies relating to a little island about which not a great deal
has ever been known, even after Napoleon, who was born there,
and stories of its fierce vendettas brought it to the attention of the
world.

III   Journal of a Tour to Corsica

The journal portion of Boswell's book on Corsica is a rather special part of his personal Journal—not, like most of it, a day-by-day
report of his life—but "a free and continued account" of what he
deemed "worthy of observation." It covers the six-week tour, the
main phase of which was his week with Paoli. The journey was an
undertaking that appeared all the more adventurous through Boswell's straightforward recording of his experiences, with no apparent
effort to sound impressive. Traveling from Leghorn (Livorna), cen-
tral west Italy, in a boat small enough for rowing, it took him two
days to reach Corsica. He was accompanied by three Corsicans
who sang devotions to the Blessed Virgin Mary at sundown and
warned him upon pain of death to leave their women alone during
his stay in their country. On the first night after reaching the island, the rains were so heavy that no one could stir abroad. The

next morning, when the rains had ceased, Boswell went to church and heard a sermon on the horrors of hell. He then started on his journey from village to village, stopping overnight in private homes or in convents (so called, but actually monasteries). He either rode a mule or traveled on foot. Once he was accompanied by two stout women who carried his baggage on their heads. It must have been disconcerting for him to notice that Corsican peasants were always armed and had a way of jumping out of coverts.

Just before reaching Corte, Paoli's seat of government, Boswell traveled through wild and mountainous country on mules equipped with cords around their necks instead of with bridles. Upon his arrival, he was accommodated in the convent where Paoli had an apartment. Since the general was in a village across the mountains at the time, Boswell occupied himself by closely scrutinizing his surroundings. He was soon impressed by what he considered the sterling qualities of the government personnel that Paoli had gathered together to bring stability to a primitive people. Boswell observed and recorded in detail the honey-making process, his surprise at finding such a large collection of books in the small university in Corte, and his visit to the jail where he talked with a female prisoner who had hired a servant to strangle a woman of whom she was jealous and with a man who had murdered his wife "at the instigation of the devil." Boswell's attention was called to the outcast hangman whose father and grandfather before him had been hangmen.

The persistent Boswell would have found his way to Paoli's presence no matter what, but his letter from Rousseau made the way easy. When he was ushered into the general's study, he found him "polite" but very reserved. "I had stood in the presence of many a prince, but I never had such a trial as in the presence of Paoli. In consequence of his being in continued danger from treachery and assassination, he formed a habit of studiously observing every new face. For ten minutes we walked backwards and forwards through the room, hardly saying a word, while he looked at me, with steadfast, keen and penetrating eye, as if he searched my very soul." With customary success, Boswell soon won over the general, and we see him being "served upon a silver salver adorned with arms of Corsica." Then, with guards marching alongside, he is mounted on Paoli's horse, which was richly decked in crimson velvet and gold lace. In a matter of hours Paoli and the incredible young Scotsman formed a friendship that endured through those years when the general, exiled from the defeated Corsica, was included among the distinguished members of Johnson's circle.

In the few days that Boswell spent with Paoli he extracted from observations and interviews one of his fullest and most successful characterizations. Out of much talk but few scenes Paoli emerges a strong, devoted, and intelligent leader; a great humanist; and a superb gentleman and man of the world. Owning a good library and having an exceptional understanding of some portions of English literature and history, as well as a competency in the classics, he was deeply concerned to see the arts and sciences flourish in Corsica. He was opposed to the typical Corsican type of revenge, the vendetta, and was aware that much had to be done to raise his people from their near—primitive state. Yet he had high regard for the strength of his countrymen, and he told several tales to illustrate this strength. When an old man came in to petition him for justice in a case involving the murder of his two sons, he wanted Boswell to listen "to this fine old man."

Boswell described the general as always briskly walking to and fro, as being too animated to remain still long enough to record his thoughts. Consequently, he sometimes had to summon a monk to write them down. As he stood still or paced about the room, he shared a variety of ideas with Boswell. He held virtue to be a strong armor and believed that God's existence could be proved, that virtuous sentiments were superior to philosophical reasoning, and that it was futile to argue about fate and free will. He enjoyed the pleasures of the imagination, thought that beasts were intelligent and could communicate, and preferred Stoicism to Epicureanism. Like many of his countrymen, he firmly believed that invisible spirits existed and that the future could be foretold through dreams.

Some of the features are in the account of Paoli that contributed to the success of the *Life of Samuel Johnson*: just the right details and incidents to arrest attention of the reader so that he can re-create in his mind the situations and scenes described, the dramatic castings, the brief character descriptions, the skillfully reported conversation, and the language that never obstructs the reader's participation by calling attention to itself.

Boswell did not merely state that the Corsicans hated rain; he showed it by pointing up the wild and rugged terrain and the usual scarcity of raincoats in the event of a downpour. His joyful abandon

on reaching the solitary inn eight miles from Corte is under-
standable, for the reader already knows that there was hardly an inn
anywhere save in the few and scattered garrison towns. We learn
step by step how the hospitable friars at Corte processed their wine;
we get more than a glimpse into the loneliness of the hangman's
life; and we are made to feel the charm and vigor of a simple existence far from the "ignoble strife" of large cities. Boswell had little
fondness for primitive outdoor life, but we share his zestful participation in it one afternoon soon after departing from Corte:

> My Corsican guides appeared so hearty, that I often got down and walk-
> ed with them, doing just what I saw them do. When we grew hungry, we
> threw stones among the thick branches of the chestnut trees which over-
> shadowed us, and in that manner we filled our pockets, and went on eating
> them with great relish; and when this made me thirsty, we lay down be-
> side of the first brook, put our mouths to the stream, and drank sufficiently.
> It was just being for a little while, one of the "prisca gens mortalium, the
> primitive race of men," who ran about the woods eating acorns and drinking
> water.

Students of Boswell seem to have overlooked the fact that five
years before publication of this book he had already recorded in
his private Journal some of Johnson's talk that was to appear thirty
years later in the *Life of Samuel Johnson*, with only a few changes
in certain instances and none in others, and that he had therefore
learned much of the art of recording conversation. For this reason,
we should guard against undue emphasis upon the *Journal of a Tour
to Corsica* as preparation for either the Hebrides Journal, his next
important book, or the *Life*. Keeping this in mind, it should be revealing to compare Boswell's methods here with those used in the
biography. The two works, of course, admit of comparison in only
a limited sense. The earlier publication is the narrative of a travel
adventure in a romantic setting, whereas the *Life* is mainly a record
of city activities and city conversation—for the most part, Johnson's.
Boswell fully recognized this difference, and in both works he
showed his artistry in skillfully adapting methods and style to materials.

The difference between the usual recording of conversation in the
Tour and that in the *Life* is therefore not due to the methods of a
young writer and those of a more experienced one but to an essential difference between the quality of Paoli's talk and that of Johnson.

To this difference we must attribute Boswell's usual employment of
the indirect method of quoting Paoli's conversation and the direct
method of preserving Johnson's exact words. The Corican general
spoke French, Italian, and sometimes broken English. His dignity
and elegance could have been lost in a too faithful record of his
speech; but Boswell found means to preserve them, as, for instance,
in the following report of a conversation, which is rounded off with
a Latin quotation:

He said he would have great pleasure in seeing the world, and enjoying
the society of the learned, and the accomplished of every country. I asked
him how with these dispositions, he could bear to be confined to an island
yet in a rude uncivilized state; and, instead of participating Attick evenings, "noctes coenaeque Deum," be in continual course of care and of danger. He replied in one line of Virgil . . .: "Vincet amor laudumque immensa
cupido." This was uttered with a fine open Italian pronunciation, and the
graceful dignity of his manner, was very noble. I wished to have a statue
taken of him at that very moment.

Paoli was a man of action and ideas; but, unlike Johnson, he was
no wit. The mirth he liked was what was "easy and unaffected,"
and he could not endure for long "the sayers of good things." It
was, then, not his wit nor even his hard common sense (which he did
have) that made his conversation attractive to his Scottish visitor;
but noble ideas and evidence of sterling character, which Boswell
somehow conveyed well at second hand: "He said the greatest happiness was not in glory but in goodness; and that Penn in his
American colony, where he had established a people in quiet and
contentment, was happier than Alexander the Great after destroying
multitudes at the conquest of Thebes." It was the unadorned, pithy
remark and a few well-chosen details that completed the picture
and brought to life both man and situation. The secret in this kind of
reporting was discerned by Johnson, who said that the difference
between the *Tour* and the *Account* is just that difference that will
always be found "between notions borrowed from without and notions generated within. Your history was copied from books; your
journal rose out of your own experience and observations. You express images which operated strongly upon yourself, and you impressed them with great force upon your readers. I know not that
I could name any narrative by which curiosity is better excited or
gratified."[6]

When Boswell left after spending several days with Paoli, he was accompanied by a giant priest who was not burdened with either knowledge or care and who sang amusing songs about the devil and the Genoese. Before Boswell left the country he watched four guards do a savage dance to the tune of Corsican airs while they sprang upon their toes, thumped their heels, and violently wheeled about. As he passed through Bastia on his way out of the country, he did nothing to discourage the rumor that he officially represented the British government for the purpose of establishing a commerce bureau in Corsica.

IV *Success and More on Corsica*

The book was a financial success, netting Boswell a hundred guineas for the copyright sold to the printing firm of Charles and Edward Dilly, which issued three editions within a year. That Boswell was now a literary success, however, meant infinitely more to him than any financial rewards. Benjamin Franklin, General Oglethorpe, and Samuel Johnson came to his lodgings in London to pay respects to the new author; and Gray and Walpole, although they made fun of the writer, praised his book. As Boswell was to observe to General Paoli, he had surely "got upon a rock in Corsica, and jumped into the middle of life.[7] At this time he must have been better known on the Continent than Samuel Johnson, and he was even to figure subsequently as one of the main characters in a romanticized novel about Paoli, which was written during the next century—*Pasquale Paoli* by Francesco Guerrazzi, an Italian writer.

Even after Boswell had returned from Corsica, had published his book, and the Corsicans had capitulated to the French, to whom the Genoese ceded the island, his Corsican enthusiasm did not diminish. Arrayed in the costume, accoutrements, and arms of a Corsican chief, he attended the Shakespeare Jubilee at Stratford-on-Avon in the fall of 1769 and distributed in the form of a broadside "Verses in the Character of a Corsican," which he later sent to a number of periodicals. The broadside carried the picture of an armed Corsican who, in twenty-three decasyllabic couplets, urged the happy Britons to come to the aid of "Liberty distressed." If this stunt fed the author's appetite for public notice, it hardly did much for the cause of freedom in the beleaguered little island.

His account of the Jubliee, published in a number of periodicals, was, nonetheless, a superb example of journalistic reporting; and it is therefore more to his credit than the episode of the Corsican chief. With habitual candor he explained his method: "I shall not follow a regular method of narrating the proceedings exactly, but just mention what made an impression upon myself: that is the best rule for every man to follow if he wishes to entertain."[8] He followed this naturalistic, but not artless, principle even down to naming a guinea as the price of a bed in crowded Stratford. Johnson noticed this principle in Boswell's account of his Corsican experiences; and it, as much as anything else, was responsible for the success of the great biography.

Once Boswell put his mind to it, he could be a tireless worker for a cause, as he was, for instance, in behalf of Archibald Douglas. In 1769, after having fed the press with numerous items about Paoli and his brave warriors and having published his *Account of Corsica*, he collected and edited a number of essays which rallied Englishmen to the support of the Corsicans—*British Essays in Favour of the Brave Corsicans*. This volume was compiled after the Genoese had surrendered all claims to authority to the French. Boswell hoped that the essays, for the most part open letters reprinted from periodicals, would prevent Great Britain from allowing the French, now that they had taken over from the Genoese, "to destroy the Corsicans, and add to their dominions one of the most considerable islands in Europe," and that it would serve as "an encouragement" to the natives in their efforts to achieve liberty.[9] The twenty essays in the book, at least three of which may have been written by Boswell, have little, if any, literary value.

CHAPTER 4

Periodical Journalist
and Political Pamphleteer

B UOYED up by his Corsican experience and his newly won
recognition as an interesting writer, Boswell in 1770 faced the
future with assurance. He cast about for means of further establishing himself in the glorious company of authors and of rising in the
world of affairs. When he returned from the Grand Tour, he sought
ways to utilize his duties at the Scottish bar, to which he had recently been called, as byways to political advancement. Between
1770 and 1785, he published a series of three periodical essays on
actors, another of seventy on a variety of subjects, and several
pamphlets dealing with current public issues. The two series of
periodical essays merited publication in the twentieth century before the discovery of the new Boswell papers and documents made
Boswell one of the literary sensations of modern times.

I Garrick and the Players

It was not politics that prompted Boswell's first literary effort of
any consequence after he began his law practice but his attachment
to the theater and his admiration for David Garrick, England's
greatest actor of the eighteenth century. In the late summer and
fall of 1770 he sent to the *London Magazine*, with which he had
managerial connections,[1] a series of three refreshing essays entitled
On the Profession of a Player.[2] Having spent much time in the
society of theatrical people and having attempted, if unsuccessfully,
to produce a play,[3] Boswell was no doubt rather well equipped to
write about acting.

His clear, forceful style bespeaks a good supply of personally
acquired knowledge; and his musings and philosophical queries into
the peculiar qualities that make for success in an actor suggest a
burning curiosity to know and understand more about the art of

acting. In the first essay, he expressed pleasure that his age eschewed the custom of the ancients in holding that players were contemptible. Acting should, in fact, be ranked as a learned profession; for it required the kind of genius displayed by David Garrick, whose recent travels on the Continent had augmented his already impressive store of ideas. In addition, the actor must have, as Garrick had, a knowledge of human nature and "all the genteel accomplishments."

The second essay is of special autobiographical interest to the student of Boswell, for it is an inquiry into one characteristic of a good actor which Boswell well knew that he himself possessed: a voluntary operation of the mind by which an actor becomes, in a sense, the character whom he represents. He sought to explain this "mysterious power" as "a kind of double feeling"—one like, for instance, that of a barrister who enters warmly into the case of a client that he knows is in the wrong. Many men in common everyday life, he continued, have had this experience. Indeed, not few in number are the illustrious men in history who have assumed "external characters without hurting their own" and have thus actually been transmuted into these characters. Boswell's Journal bears testimony to the perennial satisfaction he enjoyed from contemplating this gift in himself. He regretted that Garrick had not published his explanation of an actor's faculty of transmutation, for it was a mystery into which it would be well worthwhile to probe. This concern of his suggests that, were he living today, Boswell would perhaps enjoy reading what the existentialists have written about man's freedom of choice in relation to different modes of reality and the resulting infinite possibilities of existence.

The last of the trilogy about acting is also of special value to the inquirer into Boswell's ideas and personality and into his reading background. It contains one of the best of the author's many discussions of happiness and one of his choicest passages on death, another of his favorite subjects for speculation. He attributed the abundance of contemporary literature about acting to the popularity of the stage in his time, and he showed a knowledge of much of this literature, which he often mentioned in his Journal: essays by Addison and Steele in the *Spectator*, the *Tatler*, and the *Guardian*; Colley Cibber's *Apology for the Life of Mr. Colley Cibber, Comedian*; Theophilus Cibber's *Lives of the British Actors and Actresses*; poems about acting by Robert Lloyd, Charles Churchill, and Hugh Kelley; the monthly publication the *Dramatic Censor*; and articles in magazines and newspapers. He thus brought to his intimate knowledge of actors and acting an uncommonly full acquaintance with recent literature on drama and the theater; and what is more important, as a fresh approach to the subject, was his deep curiosity for "minute circumstances in the exercise of character upon the stage, which do not appear upon reading the poet, but must be supplied by the player from his observations of human life."

As Boswell again expressed the wish that Garrick would oblige with a treatise on acting, he experienced a curiosity that prompted him to explore the essential nature of happiness in the world, which is peculiarly discernible in the lives of players; and he easily turned from this quest to a contemplation of death, a state which he found especially difficult to associate with actors. If happiness consists in having the mind agitated, players must be the happiest of men: "They are agitated in all variety of which human nature is capable, and if the length of life, as those who are studious of metaphysical refinement maintain, is to be estimated by the time in which we have been sensible of activity of mind, the lives of players are much longer than those of any class of mortals." It is, therefore, not easy to contemplate that for players a time must come "when those features which have been so often employed to express the varieties of human emotion and passion, must be convulsed with the agonies of dissolution: when those organs of speech which have touched so many hearts must forever be dumb: when those who have animated such a multiplicity of characters, must sink into a cold sensibility . . . I fancy every one of them must say in the affecting words of my Lord Lyttleton's prologue, 'Alas! I feel I am no actor here.'"

Boswell was repeatedly moved by the wonder of mental agitation which he virtually equated with happiness, and he often expressed a kind of horror not for the terrors that death has in store for man but for its function of blotting out the felicities of life. The essays of the trilogy about the profession of a player are, therefore, not conventional treatments of the subject; and they make good reading, for Boswell, a good actor, put much of himself into them.

His chief inspiration for the essays about actors was David Garrick, who had become celebrated among London's lovers of the theater since he and Johnson had ridden together thirty-four years earlier to the city from Lichfield. Boswell, who had known the famous actor for several years, had been with him in 1769 at Stratford-on-Avon, where Garrick was steward of the Shakespeare Jubilee and where he had read "a Parcel" of verses that Boswell had written to him.[4] On this occasion Boswell wrote other complimentary verses about Garrick, which he had printed and circulated in a popular form of the day, the broadside. Many of the broadsides were ballads, sold on the streets and sung to popular tunes, that were often satires and lampoons, but sometimes eulogies, like this one of Boswell's, entitled *Verses in the Character of a Corsican* (1769), that praised his actor friend for stealing "nature's pen" where Shakespeare had dropped it.

Now, as always, they were on good terms, and Garrick later acted as one of Boswell's main supporters when he came up for election to the Literary Club.[4] A year after the appearance of the essays on players, Boswell wrote a dedication to Garrick for the Donaldson edition of Shakespeare.[5] It reads in part: "To David Garrick, Esq: You, Sir, by animating his characters on the stage, have shown the British nation the astonishing treasures of the Father of their Drama. And I even question if ever his genius was sufficiently acknowledged by the general voice till you appeared."

II *"The Hypochondriack"*

Boswell's second venture into periodical writing was the long series of essays which he published in the *London Magazine* from October, 1777, to August, 1783,[6] one appearing monthly for seventy consecutive months. Styling himself "The Hypochondriack," he remained anonymous throughout the six years. Since the papers treated a variety of subjects, many of them making either no reference at all or a very slight one to hypochondria, we would naturally ask what bearing the title had on the aim and content of the essays and why Boswell published them anonymously.

Thirty-eight years old when he sent the first number to the press, he had suffered throughout his life from intermittent serious attacks of depression, which he labeled "hypochondria"; and there were few, if any, topics he talked or wrote about more frequently. His attacks were hardly more serious than Dr. Johnson's; but, as would be expected, Boswell's complaints were louder. His firsthand knowledge and extensive reading about the ailment qualified him to write authoritatively on it. Also, he was eager to prepare installments regularly for publication as a proving ground for his ability to dis-

cipline himself emotionally; moreover, he wished to experiment
with a special project by which he could settle to his own satisfaction
his ability to succeed in this kind of writing. While on his European
tour, about fourteen years prior to the start of the series, he had
declared that he was drinking in experience as preparation for becoming a periodical essayist.

The first essay, in fact, is about periodical writing as a form of
literature, and it makes mention of hypochondria only at the end.
Allowing that the purpose of this kind of essay was to instruct and
to entertain, Boswell examined the genre first from the point of view
of the writer and then from that of the reader. He thought the essay
to be a pleasant means by which experienced authors temporarily
indisposed to sustained endeavor could avoid inactivity and by
which inexperienced writers, not yet accustomed to the discipline
of constant application necessary for the production of important
and longer books, could "strengthen their faculties." He thought
that the great variety and treatment of subject matter in this form
of prose literature was its chief attraction. Studious and indolent
readers alike could derive value from the type: the former, finding
something complete, though brief; the latter, being enticed to
read until they had acquired good habits of study "like one of a
weakly stomach, who is made to eat often and little at a time, till
his organs strengthen and he is able to take a full meal."

As Boswell pondered the relation between writers and readers,
he recalled the expansion of London's reading public to include
many persons who were not authors. Writers unmindful of this
development tended to neglect great numbers of their readers.
During Queen Anne's time, he continued, essays were produced
by "a constellation of wits"; and, since then, there had been poor
as well as excellent ones written. We ought, even so, to be convinced
that this mode of writing "has intrinsic excellence, and that mankind
are fully sensible of its value."

Finally getting around to the subject of hypochondria at the close
of his initial essay, Boswell observed that the ailment was characteristic of English people, yet was not unknown in any country; and
he bemoaned the unavailability of medicines that could effect a
cure. He promised that he would sometimes devote an essay exclusively to the distemper but that it would generally be his intention to divert "hypochondriacks" by means of contributions on
various subjects "as I can furnish from my intellectual store." Only

four of the seventy essays are devoted expressly to hypochondria: two of these are near the beginning (those of February and March, 1778); not until three years later (December, 1780) is there another; and the fourth and last (December, 1782) appears after a lapse of two years, seven months before the end of the series (August, 1783). Of the remaining sixty-six essays, the connection with the malady is slight; and, even in some of the fifteen instances where it is mentioned, its relation to the subject is often tenuous or nonexistent.

Other topics, to be sure, often have an unmistakable bearing on hypochondria. This is especially true of the essays about fear, conscience, death, and drinking. It appears that forty-nine of the seventy essays were written with no apparent thought or mention of hypochondria. Moreover, Boswell said that he wanted his papers read in "the library of the divine, in the drawing room of the matron and in the toilet of the young lady." Despite this heterogeneity of theme and of readers for whom the essays were intended, the series had a kind of unity that derived partly from the author's avowedly undertaking to cure himself from hypochondria by having a regular task to perform (which to his credit he plied faithfully), by his stated aim of helping other "hypochondriacks" through making available to them entertaining and instructive reading matter, by devoting some essays exclusively to hypochondria and others partly to it, and by maintaining a lucid expression and a pleasant tone throughout the series. Having suffered so long from the instabilities and agonies arising from the disorder and having augmented his firsthand knowledge by the written and spoken testimony of others, Boswell, while surely no Addison, presented information of real value in an interesting, lively manner. This statement is especially true about the papers on hypochondria and, probably to a lesser degree, about those on luxury, youth and age, cooking, government, criticism, words, love, marriage, memory, swearing, and religion.

Miss Margery Bailey, in her Introduction to the American edition of the essays,[7] seems inclined to minimize Boswell's literary intentions, noting his anonymity and his apparent lack of concern for literary fame. She contends that he was examining "his own faults and opinions to the exclusion of every thing else." Since this was no doubt true of many of his writings—true even to a degree of portions of his *Life of Samuel Johnson*—it has scant relevance to his purpose and method in the "Hypochondriack" papers. Evidence pointing to essentially literary objectives remains impressive. He signed the papers anonymously, but it was fairly well known who the author was; and he used the essays as a proving ground of his talents in this genre of literature.

Wishing to be the reader's "companion and friend" and not a "dreary teacher," Boswell eschewed "too much seriousness." Nor would he allow an exception even for the topic of death, complimenting himself on not having "made the awful subject more gloomy." He thought that one of the best ways to please was to cultivate the "desultory" manner, which would permit digressions from time to time. At the beginning of the first of his essays on country life, for instance, he discussed at length Dryden's use of triplets of essays—three on love, three on death, and now three on living in the country. The marked irrelevance in the opening of the essay on conscience came from overemphasis. Nearly a page and a half was devoted to the circumstances under which Cicero uttered the words making up the motto for the essay. The painstaking description of these circumstances did no more to advance the thought than would have been accomplished by the mere presentation of the motto. In his treatment of war he adhered more closely to the theme, the irrationality of war, until near the end, when, seeming to fear that he was forgetting to be desultory and would thus bore his readers, he concluded his paper with a few additional observations upon war and a description of a battle, which he had taken from the pages of Boyer's *English and French Dictionary.*

In the first of three consecutive essays on love, Boswell failed to follow a clear line of development in his ruminations on the subject. In the next he made no attempt at organization and said frankly that, instead of imposing upon himself "the task of regular system and exact order," he would "just throw out what thoughts occur to me, as if I were sitting with a friend."

The particular form of a given essay, it is true, can not always be attributed to Boswell's casual attitude toward reader and subject; at times, it was determined by the inevitable and logical breakdown of subject into parts or by the limitations of space arising from the exigences of serial publication. Examples of logical division are found in treatments of excess and change. In support of the thesis that there can be no kind of excess which is not harmful, successive paragraphs treated, in turn, excess in eating, wealth, poverty, bodily strength, power, love pleasure, and finally this particular essay, of which the reader must already have had quite enough. In regard to the effect that serial publication has on organization, the paper on similarity among authors is a case in point. Having in a previous essay (on quotations) come to the end of the space allowed before completing what he had to say, he used the opening paragraphs of the next installment (on authors) in order to finish.

Though sometimes not clearly defined, Boswell's sense of direction was never so hazy as to lead his readers into meandering paths, nor was the way ever obscured by weeds of erudition. One is always aware of where he is being led, although he is occasionally somewhat surprised to find himself on a bypath after an abrupt and unceremonious departure from the main road. When Boswell did not bother to conclude an essay, he merely ended it.

In tone and method, he reflected the neoclassical ideals of order, restraint, good manners, good taste, and good sense. Fifteen years before the beginning of the series, in fact, he wrote that he wanted his Journal to please with the "elegant ease of its language."[8] He took pains to avoid a quality of Johnson's prose which he described as "inflated Rotundity and tumified Latinity of Diction."[9] Boswell's natural preference for the amenities of sophistication and well-bred ease helped determine the tone of the essays, the quality of the prose, the contents, and to a considerable extent even their organization. The prose is direct, straightforward, and lucid.

Boswell supported generalizations with vivid comparisons, which, like Francis Bacon's, are often taken from common household or natural objects. When he adduced the testimony of authorities or used illustrations from Latin, Greek, and modern writers, he did so with smooth and easy relevance. He was seldom vulgar or over familiar, as he occasionally allowed himself to be in his Journal; but he was easy and friendly, yet dignified in tone. Except for two essays written at an earlier period and inserted into the series (one on numbers and the other on a new freezing invention), he was never flippant or impudent in manner.

Matthew Arnold's estimate of Byron's poems as loose in form but abounding in short situations, incidents, and descriptions of the highest order calls to mind a somewhat similar characteristic of the prose of the "Hypochondriack" essays. We could hardly say of this prose that it is ever of the first order, but it now and then attains a high quality in single passages. This is true, for instance, in one of the essays on hypochondria in which the style is clear and limpid and devoid of augmentation or support from authority as it achieves a rare note of sincerity and immediacy that could derive only from painful personal experience. In the essay on criticism Boswell reached a high point in his intelligent and honest vindication of the critic's function and a reasonable respect for his judgment. We can hardly remain unimpressed by the fresh point of view and lively imagination that informs his ruminations on the irrationality of war: had mankind neither seen nor been told of these "gallant exertions," and if people were therefore totally free from prejudice in favor of them, he wrote, they would be sure to

treat as fabulous or allegorical, the accounts in history, of prodigious armies being formed, of men who engaged themselves for an unlimited time, under the penalty of immediate death, to obey implicitly the orders of commanders to whom they were not attached either by affection or by interest; that those armies were sometimes led with toilsome expedition over vast tracts of land, sometimes crowded into ships, and obliged to endure tedious, unhealthy and perilous voyages; and that the purpose of all this toil and danger was not to obtain any comfort or pleasure, but to be in a situation to encounter other armies; and that those opposite multitudes the individuals of which had no cause of quarrel, no ill-will to each other, continued for hours engaged with patient and obstinate perseverance, while thousands were slain, and thousands crushed and mangled by diversity of wounds.[10]

Now Boswell was under no illusion about the merit of his performance. At times he would write with few notes, he said, and occasionally with none. In order to work under high pressure, he purposely waited until shortly before time for publication of each essay before beginning to write. The "Hypochondriack" had to plead what was "peculiar to his own cast of mind, a hurry of spirits." Furthermore, he stated quite frankly, he knew he could never write a *Spectator* or a *Rambler*.

III *Political Pamphleteer and Scottish Patriot*

No sooner had Boswell put up his lawyer's shingle in 1766 than he presented himself to the elder William Pitt, the prime minister, in behalf of the Corsicans; and he bided his time until such issues arose in national affairs that afforded just the opportunities that he was seeking as a lawyer and as a writer with political ambitions. He utilized several opportunities to assure his fellow countrymen of his patriotism and good will and thus to gain support of his Ayrshire constituency for a seat in Parliament: a country-wide bankruptcy, a constitutional dispute in the General Assembly of the Church of Scotland, a famous court contest involving literary property of Edinburgh publishers, a bill in Parliament to transfer the government of the East India Company from the crown to private hands, and a parliamentary move to decrease the number of judges in the Scottish Court of Session. Each of these causes elicited from Boswell a pamphlet, an article, or an open letter to the newspapers.

This period was indeed, as literary historians have not sufficiently recognized, Boswell's most Scottish one; and, paradoxically, it was a time when he was setting down the main planks of the foundation upon which he would attempt with pitiful ineffectiveness to build his London life in the years ahead. His deep pride in the abiding greatness of Scottish history and character persisted, but his love for Scotland never equaled the irresistible fascination of London life and English manners. Many were the times when he doggedly told himself that he could have both Ayrshire and London—and how might he better accomplish this and resolve the tension than by winning a seat in Parliament? With such an end in view, he often employed his time and pen during this period when he continued to reside in Scotland but traveled to London for rather frequent and prolonged sojourns. It should not be overlooked that virtually at the outset of this period (in 1773) Boswell and Johnson made their delightful three-month excursion into Scotland and the Hebrides Islands off Scotland's west coast and later published journals about the tour.

Boswell's twenty-three-page pamphlet, *Reflections on the Late Alarming Bankruptcies* (1772), was occasioned by a bankruptcy that nearly destroyed Scotland's meager economy. It is interesting mainly for its unrestrained vindication of rank and subordination as stabilizing forces in society and for its doleful lament on the passing of gentility in Scotland. Boswell distinguished between the true bankers, on whom depend the vigor and stability of a nation, and the false ones, who have squandered other people's money, strut in "borrowed feathers," and live in a fashion unbecoming of men of low rank. He warned the latter to pay when payment is due; or, if they must strut, they were to do so in prison. He did not limit his censure to bankers but let it fall as well on the citizens who were only too content to acquiesce in the leveling of social distinctions that was accelerated after the seat of government was moved to Lon-

don, carrying with it most of the people of fashion. The disappear-
ance of subordination as an organizing principle of society was, in
fact, the first cause of the bankruptcies.

Boswell rallied against the upstarts who spend more money in a
week than their fathers did in a year, while the true gentry, for whom
the fathers of these upstarts worked as servants, were associating
equally with them. He comforted himself with the thought that the
distinction of good birth was not a marketable commodity and
therefore could not be acquired by low-born, ill-bred speculators.
Since, nevertheless, the low could not rise, the high were sinking to
their level. This decline was seen in the heavy-feasting and hard-
drinking parties that had become common in Scotland. Furthermore, manners had become coarse, and the drawing rooms were like
convents; for the men were seldom seen unless in an intoxicated
condition in some public place.

The bankruptcies, according to Boswell, were caused not only by
the collapse of the class system but by the increase in the number
of debts from extravagant living and from the craze of merchants,
tradesmen, farmers, and laborers to become rich soon. Extensive
borrowing resulted in mass circulation of paper ("the appearance of
strength without reality"). Boswell appealed to three classes of
readers to help out in this crisis: those who were able to pay and
should, therefore, be forced to pay their creditors; those who could
not pay immediately but should candidly explain why to their creditors; and those who could not pay now or would ever be able to do
so. Anyone in the last category should make his insolvency known
and cease to borrow. Boswell ended with the hope that the bankruptcies, despite their distressing consequences to many individuals,
would help restore the proper regard for thrift, subordination, and
other stabilizing forces.

In April of the year that saw this pamphlet on the economic crisis,
Boswell continued his endeavors for the Scottish cause with an ar-
ticle, published in two installments in *The Scots Magazine*, entitled
*A Sketch of the Constitution of the Church of Scotland, and the
State of the Parties in it at Present; with specimens of Oratory of
Some of the most distinguished Members of that Church now
living.*[11] Again he was concerned with the preservation of national
dignity and traditions. While he preferred the more ceremonial
Church of England to his national church, he praised the latter for

its constitution, which "the greatest lovers of liberty and equality must admire"; and he lauded the General Assembly of the Church of his fathers as "perhaps the most learned assembly of men that now meet for deliberation as a court of tribunal or legislative body." His editorial work for this group was again seen in the *Debates of the General Assembly of the Church of Scotland*, which he sent to the *London Magazine* a year later.

Boswell's last publication of the 1770's that was devoted to the Scottish cause was a pamphlet in which his hand was primarily that of compiler: *The Decision of the Court on Literary Property* (1774). He must have welcomed another opportunity to rally to the support of his countrymen, which came in the form of a lawsuit involving Alexander Donaldson and other Edinburgh publishers that were lined up defensively against the London publishers. The case affords a glimpse into an interesting development in eighteenth-century bookselling and publishing and into the relationship between publisher and author. Edinburgh publishers would print cheap editions of books that had already been published in London, thus bypassing the copyright law. Donaldson settled in London and made a fortune on these cheap editions. Called "Great Donaldson" and the "prodigious vendor" because of his immense business, he introduced the young aspiring writers Boswell and Erskine to other Paternoster Row booksellers, whom, as Boswell put it, he "engaged to befriend us."

The London publishers maintained that an author's copyright existed in perpetuity and that therefore the Edinburgh publishers, in selling both in Edinburgh and in London reprinted editions of standard works beyond the period specified in the statutes on copyrights, were violating the law. Boswell's pamphlet is an account of the case in the Scottish Court of Session in which Boswell's father participated as one of the eleven judges who ruled that the statutes on copyrights did not apply in Scotland, a decision later upheld in the House of Lords.

Boswell did not again bestir himself for his countrymen until nine years later, when the East India Bill, introduced in the House of Commons by Charles Fox, became the occasion of another pamphlet and therefore another chance for him to assert his leadership. This bill sought to transfer, in effect, the control of the affairs of a virtual dominion to a company of traders; for the political government, according to the provisions of the bill, would pass from the director of the East India Company, who had been operating under royal charter, to a board of seven commissioners. Boswell vigorously attacked this proposed legislation in his *Letter to the People of Scotland on the Present State of the Nation* (1783), charging that such a shift of power and authority would be destructive of both private property and constitutional monarchy. His purpose was not to stir up sentiment in defeat of the bill, since it had already been turned down in the House of Lords, but to recommend that the Scottish people, in organized groups and individually, should express their great satisfaction that it had been rejected. This forty-page pamphlet is perhaps the most interesting and spirited assertion of Boswell's support of the American rebellion, and it is at the same time a strong declaration of his feudal ideas on hereditary royal prerogative.

In the opening paragraphs he scolded his fellow Scotsmen for being indifferent to public affairs, and especially for their acquiescence in and tacit approval of the control of the king's American subjects by his British subjects. It was unjust, he wrote, because Americans were being taxed without the consent of their representatives; and it was inexpedient because all Americans were not cowards. He could not agree with the one man in the world for whom he had greatest respect, Samuel Johnson, who had written that taxation was not tyranny. The king, Boswell claimed, had been advised by evil counselors. Americans would be willing to submit to him but not to his subjects.

The bill, Boswell went on to say, would have been destructive of the security of private property and of the constitution. For over two centuries the East India Company, under charter from the crown, had controlled the lands, books, records, and properties which, had the bill succeeded, would have passed into the hands of a set of men not of the king's appointment. Such a transference would, therefore, have been a violation of the royal prerogative. Boswell cited Charles I, who forbade Parliament to waste time with bills to which he would not give his assent, and even William, who was elected to the throne, would, on occasion, withhold the royal hand from bills that had been passed by both Houses. Boswell's heart was in this attack on the East India Bill. He inherited his reverence for charters; for, as he said near the close of the pamphlet,

he held an estate that had been transmitted to him through his ancestors "by charters from a series of Kings." Not wanting to appear
too carried away with Tory sentiments, he was careful to point out
that his veneration of monarchy was not inconsistent with "genuine
feelings of liberty," and that, while he was a Tory, he was not a
slave. He then quoted Samuel Johnson's distinction between a Whig
and a Tory: "there is but a shade of difference between a moderate
Whig and a spirited Tory, between reasonable men of each party."

Boswell's pamphlet on the East India Bill failed in its intended
aim of establishing himself as leader of his Ayrshire constituency, to
whom he was looking for a seat in Parliament in the coming general
elections; but he found occasion for another pamphlet and for
another opportunity to further his political ambitions when a bill
was introduced in the House of Commons in April, 1785, that would
reduce from fifteen to ten the number of judges in the Scottish
Court of Session. As before, he again appealed to the loyalty of his
compatriots in *A Letter to the People of Scotland on the Alarming
Attempt to Infringe the Articles of Union and Introduce a Most
Pernicious Innovation by Diminishing the Number of Lords of Session* (1785).

Justice this time, not the crown itself, was in danger. Without con-
sulting his fellow countrymen, Henry Dundas, the young ambitious
solicitor general and a few other Scots whom he lavishly entertained
had suddenly and secretly introduced the bill, Boswell charged,
and thus threatened to undermine the chief judicial body in the
land. He explained that, since Scotland had no juries in civil cases,
this court was the chief protection against unjust persecutions and
that the number of judges should remain what it had been for two
hundred and fifty-three years unless by consent of the people of
Scotland.

Boswell considered a reduction of judges a dangerous innovation
not only in his country's judicial system but in the social life of its
capital. Already, he said, the chief society of Edinburgh was composed of lawyers who ruled the theater and made balls for the ladies.
If the proposed bill were successful, the remaining judges' salaries
would increase, and the Scottish Bench would become an *etat*, a
rank. Boswell's personal, intimate touch is in evidence in the rest
of the pamphlet as we see him invoking the aid of numerous members of Parliament, including the notorious John Wilkes, whose

pleasant society he said he could not resist despite his biting attacks on Scotland. He imagined William Pitt, the crown's second minister, sending for Dundas and blasting at him, "Dundas, for shame, I'll hear no more of this Court of Sessions job!"

Boswell's references became increasingly personal: he mentioned his own interest in Parliament, Goldsmith's introducing him to Sir Joshua Reynolds, and his ability to laugh with persons of different political and religious persuasions; he also proudly claimed that his ancestor Thomas Boswell received the charter for the family estate from James IV for fighting against the English. He was unable to find any advantages which Scotland had derived from her recent union with England. In fact, he wrote, Scotland had lost her spirit, and her growth had been hampered through discontinuance of her parliament. A similar concern for Scotland's welfare and prestige is noticeable in a letter to *Gentleman's Magazine*[12] expressing regret that the recent edition of the *Biographical Dictionary* omitted the names of such Scots authors as Alan Ramsay and Alexander Montgomerie.

Boswell continued in his blunderings and gropings for political recognition until the closing months of his life, but at no period were his political activities so concentrated as during these fifteen years from 1770 until 1785. At no time before or afterward did he devote so much of his energies to the cultivation of good will among his Scots compatriots. Not again was he to publish so many items, both separately and in periodicals, devoted to the Scots' cause and to politics.

The death of Johnson in 1784 left Boswell free to publish his *Journal of a Tour to the Hebrides* and *The Life of Samuel Johnson*, the first serving as a kind of sensational preview of the second. He wistfully turned his eyes away from Scotland with divided emotions. Had he resolved the conflict within by assuming his role as the new laird of Auchinleck, thereby achieving stability and dignity for himself and family, his great biography would hardly have seen the light of day. He loved London well. Who can say he loved it unwisely?

CHAPTER 5

Hebrides and the Aftermath

T HE LAST ten years of Boswell's life, barring a few bright spots, were the most dismal in his personal history. Nevertheless, they saw the completion of the two books that secured him a place in literature among the immortals. In no previous period had he been so uprooted, so often a victim of fears and doubts, and so close to desperation. In 1788, after the second year, he gave up the recordship of Carlisle, the highest political office he was able to attain, because Carlisle was too far from London. His efforts to present his native Ayrshire in Parliament met with failure, which he attributed mainly to outspoken utterances in his second *Letter to the People of Scotland* (1785).[1] Revealing its author as "ambitious" but "uncorrupted," it elicited from his friend Lord Mounstuart a remark that Boswell considered complimentary: "I would do anything for you but bring you into Parliament."[2]

While Boswell had little difficulty managing to be called to the English bar, the decision to practice in London and thus forego a comfortable, decent life on his recently inherited ancestral estate cost him many agonizing hours. The failure of his law practice in the English capital brought on additional weeks and months of gnawing indecisions as to whether he should not, after all, abandon his English ambitions and return to Scotland. The pleasure he anticipated from the success of his *Journal of a Tour to the Hebrides* (1785) was canceled out by rancorous responses from some of his acquaintances.

He had already suffered the loss of his friend and counselor, Samuel Johnson; and now his loneliness and personal inadequacy were accentuated by the death of his wife, whom he greatly valued but consistently neglected. Left with five children to take care of, he divided his time between them, his dissipations, his literary and social relationships (which surprisingly enough he maintained throughout this period with little apparent effort), and work on the *Life of Johnson*. He knew that his achievement would be distinguished, but this knowledge brought him little joy. Not yet in his middle fifties, his fire was nearly out. Never again would he experience a thrill such as his book on Corsica had given him in his giddy late twenties.

I   *The Journal of a Tour to the Hebrides*

Boswell and Johnson had made their journey into western Scotland and the Hebrides in the late summer and fall of 1773. The account that Boswell wrote of it was just a part, but a special part, of the virtually continuous Journal that he had been keeping for a number of years and was to continue until shortly before his death. *The Journal of a Tour to the Hebrides* is the published version of this Journal which Boswell wrote during the three months that the two men spent together on the trip, although he was neither recording to include the account in the *Life of Johnson* as a full unit nor writing for the purpose of publishing this part of his Journal separately. It was this very Journal, however, that he later decided to present to the public: "I will not expand the text in any considerable degree, though I may occasionally supply a word to complete the sense, as I fill up the blanks of abbreviation in the writing; neither of which can be said to change the genuine Journal."[3]

The bulk of the book was as suggested, written while the trip was in progress: "I am slow to believe any man's memory, at the distance of several years, can preserve facts or sayings with such fidelity as may be done by writing them down when they are recent, and I beg it may be remembered that it is not upon Memory, but what was written at the time, that the authenticity of my Journal rests." The writing of the Journal itself, was, in fact, a part of the experience reported on; and, at times, it greatly interfered with the social intercourse of the travelers. Boswell recorded in his entry for September 19, for instance, that his Journal kept him from Johnson's company: "He asked me today how it happened that we were so little together. I told him, my Journal took much time. Yet, in reflection it appeared strange to me, that although I will run from one end of London to another, to pass one hour with him I should omit to seize any spare time to be in his company, when I am settled in the same house with him."

When Johnson decided to publish his *Journey to the Western Islands of Scotland,* which came from the press in 1775, about a year after the completion of the trip, Boswell wanted to run his Journal along with it as a supplement; but he received no encouragement from Johnson. "Between ourselves," Boswell confided to Temple, "he is not apt to encourage one to share reputation with himself."[4] However, Boswell's book saw a second edition within three months and a third the next year; it was ten years before Johnson's was issued the second time.

Johnson's *Journey*, which was more in the tradition of books of travel and exploration, a popular genre of the age, is not so much the record of a jaunt as a description of places visited and an account of the customs of the people; much information in it was obtained from outside research. Boswell's *Tour*, on the other hand, is a combination of personal journal and biography, covering, nevertheless, the same travel experience. Slighting over the geographical, historical, and sociological aspects of the Hebrides, Boswell gave an enthusiastic, warmhearted record of the expressions of a great personality on the rarest holiday of his life—in fact, as he himself termed it, "a dramatic sketch—the account of the transit of Johnson over the Caledonian Hemisphere."[5] Boswell's was a better book than Johnson's, in fact, mainly because it had more of Johnson in it.

In introductory comments Boswell gave a remarkably comprehensive, though brief, sketch of Johnson's personality, character, and physical appearance. He told of his great qualities of mind and spirit and of the occasional convulsive seizures that made his head and body shake as if he had palsy or Saint Vitus's dance. He then recounts their experiences in the Scottish capital prior to their departure for northern Scotland and the Hebrides, a group of islands off the western coast of Scotland. When Boswell met the recently arrived Johnson at Cannongate in Edinburgh, he hoped that his Scotland would put her best foot forward to meet the distinguished stranger, but her worst one intruded itself at the outset. For, as he and Johnson walked arm in arm from Boyd's Inn up High Street to Boswell's house in James Court, where Mrs. Boswell was preparing tea for them, he was embarrassed that Johnson had to be assailed with the evening effluvia of Edinburgh: the stench of uncovered sewers in the section of the city known as "the old town."

It was not long before things brightened, and Boswell was able to feel a pride in the quality of the company that he had rounded up for Johnson's entertainment in the Scottish capital. Handpicked for the purpose were the banker Sir William Forbes, the judge Lord Chief Baron Orde, the duchess of Douglas, the educator Dr. William

Robertson, and the distinguished clergyman Dr. Alexander Webster.

Johnson had come to Edinburgh on Saturday, August 14. Accompanied by Boswell's stately Bohemian servant, they set out in a postchaise for the north on the next Wednesday, arriving at St. Andrews the same night. From there they proceeded up the east coast and through Aberdeen. Just before reaching the northern coast, they went west until they arrived at Fort George. From there they traveled southwest to Anoch and then west to the northern Hebrides. On their return journey through the southern Hebrides, they went southeast to Auchinleck, Boswell's ancestral home, where they remained five days and where, in what must have been an awful moment, Boswell introduced Johnson to his father. For two days they journeyed to Edinburgh, arriving there on November 9, after an absence of eighty-three days. During the next nine days Johnson met more relatives and friends of Boswell and then set out for London.

Differing emphases of Johnson's and Boswell's versions of the jaunt and the reasons for the greater popularity of Boswell's book may be discerned by comparing their accounts of the visit to Lord Monboddo's estate just outside of Montrose, of which Johnson wrote: "Early in the afternoon Mr. Boswell observed that we were at no great distance from the house of Lord Monboddo. The magnetism of his conversation easily drew us out of our way, and the entertainment which we received would have been sufficient recompense for a much greater deviation."[6] With his keen scent for the dramatic, Boswell recalled that Johnson and Monboddo did not love each other; but he was nevertheless eager to bring them together. He canvassed Johnson's feelings about the matter and found him willing to go to Monboddo's place, and then he sent his servant Joseph ahead with a letter to the Scotsman telling him that Johnson was coming two miles out of his way to see him.

Lord Monboddo courteously received them at the gate, pointed to the arms on the house, and said it was of the Douglas family, of whom his great-grandmother was a member. He then said that their ancestors lived in such houses and that they were better men than he and Johnson. Johnson objected to this observation and asserted that they were equally strong and even wiser than their ancestors. "This was an assault upon one of Lord Monboddo's dogmas, and I was afraid there would have been a violent altercation in the very close, before we got into the house. But his lordship is distinguished not only for 'ancient metaphysicks,' but for ancient politesse, 'la vielle coeur,' and he made no reply. They talked of emigration, Homer, history of manners, biography, Pope, state of learning in Scotland and England."[7]

We see in their respective treatments of the island of Skye another, among many, of the contrasts between the intentions and methods of the two writers. Johnson discussed the type of life on the island and then took a short excursion into the history of the place, utilizing as he went along a considerable amount of research on the weather, soil, agriculture; on the kinds of farms, houses, and gardens; as well as on the manners, social classes, domestic servants, dress, conversation, religion and superstition, second sight, and language. This documentary treatment of Highland life was his longest sustained discussion of any subject in the book.

The account occupying the greatest amount of space in Boswell's *Tour* was also occasioned by the visit to the island of Skye. While there, he slept in the same room in Flora Macdonald's house where Prince Charles, grandson of James II, had slept when in 1746 that celebrated woman assisted the Bonnie Prince Charlie in his escape from Britain to France during the Jacobite uprising. Boswell's digression is an engaging account of this adventuresome and romantic episode. He responded on this occasion, as he usually did, principally to the human and dramatic elements in the situation. He could not give, as could Johnson, detailed descriptions of what he saw. "I find great difficulty in describing visible objects." He admitted as he attempted to describe a recessed cave on the rocky north end of Raasay.

The Journal of a Tour to the Hebrides is by far Boswell's best sustained piece of writing, if viewed singly as a unit of Boswell's own story, as part of the memoirs of Johnson (as it is treated in two modern editions of the *Life*), or as travel literature. It is thrice excellent as a remarkable combination of the three.

As we have indicated, the focus was often on Johnson, as, for instance, when Boswell and Johnson walked together up High Street in Edinburgh; when for three days Boswell entertained Johnson in Edinburgh; when he escorted his guest about Auchinleck, his father's estate; when with his keen scent for dramatic, which he later used in bringing Wilkes and Johnson together, he eagerly arranged a meeting of Johnson with Lord Monboddo; when at Aberdeen, St. Andrews, Fort George, and wherever he could, he gathered together the informed, the learned, and the witty; when conversations were between Johnson and Boswell alone; and when in the house of Miss Flora Macdonald, where Johnson's lying in the bed in which Prince Charles lay struck Boswell "with such a group of ideas as it is not easy to describe."

At times Boswell's focus was on sheer adventure. When Boswell and Johnson took to their boat, the dark coast of Skye behind them looked like huge rocks in the dusk, and the singing of boatmen sounded like wild Indians; when they landed at night with no horses or other conveyances, they had to carry their own baggage with only one star for light. While they were on the boat bound for Coll, the sparks from the peat fire were menacingly flying about the gunpowder; and the immense billows were crashing against the vessel, which they were told had once listed within an inch of the water. As they hiked to the top of a high hill in the rocky country of Raasay, they ate cold mutton and cheese, drank brandy and punch, sang Highland songs, and danced the reel.

Johnson often read Boswell's Journal while it was in the process of being written, and one day we find him actually correcting mistakes that Boswell had made in reporting his conversation. On another occasion: "He came into my room this morning before breakfast, to read my Journal, which he had done all along. He often before said, 'I take great delight in reading it.' Today he said 'You improve: it grows better and better. . . . It might be printed were the subject fit for printing.'" Not all of the published *Tour*, however, represents what was recorded on the spot; for here and there are additions, observations, and comments that were written just prior to publication twelve years afterward. For example, when Boswell and Johnson were speculating about the behavior of Sir David Dalrymple in the event that they should disappoint him at dinner, Johnson engaged in a little playful burlesque of how that gentleman would be expected to demean himself; but, in recalling the incident and Johnson's words on the occasion, Boswell wrote: "at a distance of almost twelve years, I cannot pretend to recollect all the precise words." He looked in retrospect at his father's and Johnson's altercations on Whiggism, Presbyterianism, Toryism, and Episcopacy; and he referred to the deaths of both, who not until a number of years after the jaunt into the Hebrides were "met in a place where there is no room for Whiggism."

In noticing these additions to the original Journal, we might keep in mind references in the *Tour* to Johnson's published *Journey*, which came off the press *after* Boswell had written down his account of the vacation in Scotland. Furthermore, Boswell had not read the *Journey* until it was published. This he regretted; for, had he seen the manuscript in time, he wrote, he would have suggested to its author that he refrain from giving in his *Journey* the impression that the absence of pulleys on the windows at the inn in Banff was a condition typical in Scotland. In his entry for November 4, he corrected Johnson's explanation of the word *Auchinleck*, and there are other references to Johnson's accounts of places visited. In fact, at the end of the *Tour*, Boswell appended letters from Dalrymple and other Scotsmen in praise of the *Journey*.

Additions to the original Journal may be seen also in the revisions that were made as it was being prepared for the press. Professor Pottle has pointed out in his Preface to the Yale edition of the *Tour*[8] that Boswell made quite a number of changes in the original Journal. He deleted many passages either for prudence or for shortening the book; he rewrote some sections; and he added words or whole paragraphs, usually of comment. The printed version, as a result, is a more finished work. The conversations were rewritten as direct quotations rather than as indirect ones, and careful editing has shifted the focus more on Johnson. Powell in the Preface to his revision of the Hill edition[9] also called attention to changes that Boswell made in his Journal before going to press.

Many of these revisions were at the suggestion of Edmond Malone, who, though he had met Boswell at Sir Joshua Reynolds's as early as 1781,[10] had not come to know him well until several years later. Having seen by chance a sheet of the *Tour* at Baldwin's printing house, Malone was so impressed with Boswell's style that he took means to become better acquainted with him.[11] This was a lucky day for Boswell and for English literary history; for, as a reading of the Private Papers covering the years 1790 and 1791 strongly suggests, the *Life of Samuel Johnson* might never have come from the press had it not been for Malone's patience, understanding, and unselfish assistance. On April 29, 1785, we find Boswell dining with Malone and on the next day arranging with Dilly for the printing of the *Tour*.[12] On June 4, he recorded in his Journal that he had worked "almost all forenoon with Malone revising Hebrides."[13] Boswell was pleased to acknowledge this help in his dedication to Malone: "You have obligingly taken the trouble to peruse the orig-

inal manuscript of this Tour, and can vouch for the strict fidelity of
the present publication. Your literary alliance with our much lamented friend, in consequence of having undertaken to render one of his
labours more complete, by your edition of Shakespeare, a work
which I am confident will not disappoint the expectations of the
public, gives you another claim."[14] Malone also superintended
the first part of the second edition when its printing was in process because Boswell was in Scotland at the time.

II   *Success Without Triumph*

Despite the success of Boswell's *Tour*, it provoked some unfavorable reactions, mainly because of offensive references to a number
of persons. Mrs. Hanna More and others complained about the
way in which he had treated certain celebrities, but the angriest
expressions came from Mrs. Piozzi and Lord Macdonald. It seems
that Mrs. Piozzi saw the *Tour* in manuscript and objected to the
passage in which Boswell quoted Johnson as saying that she (then
Mrs. Thrale) could not "get through" Mrs. Montague's *Essay on
Shakespeare;* and she added a postscript to her *Anecdotes,* when
preparing it for the press, in which she denied this difficulty. Boswell, seeing the postscript just before publication of his *Tour,* answered it in a footnote entry in which he replied that not he, Beauclerk, nor Mrs. Thrale could get through the book; furthermore,
he noted that, when Mrs. Thrale had read this passage in his Journal
several years ago, she had not objected to it.[15]
One of the most offensive improprieties in the *Tour* was Boswell's
account of what he deemed flaws in the hospitality of Sir Alexander
Macdonald, later Lord Macdonald. He quoted a previous visitor to
Lord Macdonald's as agreeing that the punch bowl on the table was
handsome but not full and that Lord Macdonald was "totally unfit"
to be chief of a Highland clan because of his treatment of the tenants, who, on account of high rents, were compelled to emigrate to
America. In a letter to *Gentleman's Magazine,*[16] Boswell denied
that Lord Macdonald had forced him to suppress certain passages
in the *Tour.* His fate, nevertheless, hung in the balance during the
week when it appeared that his indiscretions would bring him to a
duel with that gentleman.[17] In his advertisement to the third edition
Boswell wrote that he had refrained from answering "the animad-
versions in the periodical Journals of criticism, and in the numerous

publications to which my book has given rise."[18] He was unable, nevertheless, to resist making a few counterattacks in this edition.

Lampoons posted in public places, commonly known as pasquinades, and caricatures freely distributed about town in ridicule of Boswell intensified the unpleasantness of his circumstances. One of the caricatures, called "Johnson's Ghost," depicted the Rambler reproaching the frightened Boswell.[19] An acquaintance of the biographer, writing of him at this time but sending his description to *Gentleman's Magazine* several years later, suggested additional causes of his wretchedness to be excessive conviviality and flightiness, resulting in the failure of his law practice first in Scotland and then in England.[20] Since publication of his *Tour of the Hebrides*, which, according to the articles, exhibited him as "the minute recorder and retailer of whatever careless conversation might have passed between persons of any eminence in his presence," Boswell had been viewed with "a general alarm" that had injured his practice at the bar and also some of his social relationships.

For all Boswell's pains in preserving the talk of the distinguished lexicographer and the wit and wisdom of many of England's brightest minds, such was his reward. Furthermore, what thanks had he received from Johnson himself, who, it would sometimes appear, had dropped him for the Thrales? A pent-up bitterness for Mrs. Thrale and a renewed resentment against the deceased Dr. Johnson were aggravated by publication in 1788 of Mrs. Thrale's edition of *The Letters of Samuel Johnson*,[21] in which Boswell found:

proof of his fawning on a woman whom he did not esteem, because he had luxurious living in her husband's home; and in order that this fawning might not be counteracted, treating me and other friends much more lightly than we had reason to expect. This publication cooled my warmth of enthusiasm for "my illustrious friend" a good deal. I felt myself degraded from the consequence of ancient Baron to the state of an humble attendant on an Author; and what vexed me, thought my collecting so much of his conversation had made the world shun me as a dangerous companion.[22]

This passage from his Journal partly explains how Boswell four years earlier could actually have brought forth the most incredible of all his writings, the *Ode by Dr. Samuel Johnson to Mrs. Thrale, Upon Their Supposed Approaching Nuptials* (1784), in the Preface of which the "editor," certainly Boswell, stated flatly that there was between Mrs. Thrale and Johnson "no over-delicate niceness, but truly the plainest familiarity." He then quoted from their letters, which, it appears, had been privately printed (for in this Preface, he referred to "a collection of their letters, which is extant, and had been put forth in print by herself"). The penultimate stanza ridiculously reads (as if written by Johnson):

> Five daughters by a former spouse
>   Shall match with nobles of the land;
> The fruit of our more fervent vows
>   A pillar of the state shall stand.

We know that Boswell wrote this ode, for he refers to it as his in two of his letters and in his published Journal.[23] It is nevertheless difficult to conceive that his resentment against Johnson would bring him to the point of descending to such a device.

While we must not dismiss this episode in evaluating their relationship, it should not be interpreted as the final expression of Boswell's feelings about his valued friend. Percy Fitzgerald in his *Boswell's Autobiography* (1912) developed the thesis that the rift between the two men was irreparable, but the evidence for Boswell's continuing regard for Johnson during Johnson's life and until his own death is easily adducible from Boswell's letters and Journals.

The success of *The Journal of a Tour to the Hebrides*, then, must have contributed little, if anything, to Boswell's well-being during the interim between the *Tour* and the *Life*. Having already agonized over the decision to leave Edinburgh and to stake his career in London, he now spent additional months trying to decide whether to remain in the English capital and to continue practicing law there. On October 15, 1787, he wrote in his Journal: "Shrunk from the thought of returning to Edinburgh yet did not see how I could go on in London." He regretted that his enthusiasm for his family and for Auchinleck had abated since he "plunged in the wide speculative scene of English ambition." Having had unpleasant encounters with Eglinton and others of his countrymen, he felt that they "almost shunned me, from an overcharged representation of my partiality to England." He would time and again set out from his quarters in Westminster with the almost certain knowledge that this day would be like all the rest: he would fail to get a case.

Boswell was nevertheless comforted by the knowledge that, in remaining in London, he was acquiring "an accession of ideas" and that he was managing with Malone's help to take some time out from his socializing and dissipations to work on the *Life*. He would regularly attend meetings of the Literary Club, often sitting as president. Bennet Langton, John Courtenay, Sir Joshua Reynolds, Edmund Burke, Edmond Malone, and the Bishop of St. Asaph were usually present. Yet, he recorded of the meeting on June 12, 1787, that there was "no force, no brilliance; nothing as when Johnson, Goldsmith, or Garrick were with us." Furthermore, Boswell no longer took an interest in motivating conversation; he was suffering from what he generally termed "an insipid dreariness."

III   *Rival Biographers*

His troubles with rival biographers at this time did not help matters. We have already noticed the friction between him and Mme Piozzi upon completion of the *Tour*. More of this was to be occasioned by the forthcoming *Life*. And now, as Boswell was preparing his manuscript for the biography, he was annoyed by the appearance of her *Letters of Dr. Samuel Johnson* in 1788 and by Sir John Hawkins's *Life of Dr. Samuel Johnson* the previous year. Boswell viewed both books as encroachments on a domain to which he claimed priority.

He was by no means universally thought of as the best person to write Johnson's life. There were others more favorably considered, including Edmond Malone, the distinguished Shakespearean editor; Bishop Thomas Percy, known best as editor of *Reliques of Ancient Poetry;* Sir William Scott, intimate friend of Johnson and member of Parliament; and Sir John Hawkins, author of a valuable history of music and an original member of Johnson's famous Literary Club. A friend of Sir William Scott wrote to him anxiously soliciting his consent to write the biography. Hawkins and Boswell were certainly not equal to the task, so thought Scott's friend, for one was "a pedant" and the other "a puppy." He therefore urged Sir William to rescue Johnson's memory from "such mean hands."[24] The booksellers of London, nearly fifty in number, entertained a better opinion of Sir John Hawkins; for they selected him as Johnson's official biographer.

Hawkins's book evoked from Boswell and his friends an immediate and uncomfortable reaction. At a meeting of the Literary
Club, one member was so incensed against Sir John that he seemed
determined to attack him. Edmond Malone at this same meeting
suggested that a "solemn protest be drawn up and signed by Dr.
Johnson's friends, to go down to Posterity, declaring that Hawkins'
was a false and injurious Account."[25] King George III was of the
same opinion. When in "full suit of black clothes" Boswell went
to the King's Levee on May 11, 1787, His Majesty "accosted" him
"with a pleasing look," asking how his writing was progressing:
"Boswell. 'Pretty well, Sir.' King. 'When will you be done?' Boswell.
'It will be some time yet . . . I have a good deal to do to correct Sir
John Hawkins.' King. 'I believe he has made many mistakes.'
Boswell. 'A good many, Sir, and very injurious to my good friend.'
King. 'I do not believe Dr. Johnson was so found of low company in
the latter part of his life as Sir John Hawkins represents (describes,
or some such word).' "[26]

It is surprising that Boswell failed to send any items to the newspapers in protest against Hawkins's book. He was, nevertheless,
planning to answer him in his own book on Johnson; and he was
counting on Hawkins's being alive when the book came off the
press so that he could read the censures against himself. Even so,
it would be interesting to know why Boswell refrained from openly
attacking him earlier. We know that Sir John had been well liked
by Johnson—in fact, he was not only one of the original members
of the Literary Club but one of Johnson's executors.

Boswell's account of his visit to Hawkins's home for the purpose
of obtaining some of Johnson's papers seems to suggest an odd kind
of respect for the man. When he called on Sir John, he had with
him a letter from Francis Barber, Johnson's Negro servant (to whom
Johnson had willed most of his belongings), authorizing him to
demand certain of Johnson's papers. He found the gentleman "with
a crimson velvet cap on," and they conducted their business in
"perfect good humor." Boswell gave the knight a receipt for three
pamphlets, three diplomas from Dublin and Oxford, and a few
papers. "We sat more severely opposite to each other in armchairs,
and I declare, he talked so well, and with such a courteous formal-
ity, that every five minutes I unloosed a knot of the critical cat
o'nine tails which I had prepared for him."[27] There was only a brief
allusion, and that in good humor, to Hawkins's slighting Boswell

in his biography with a mere reference to him as "Mr. Boswell, a native of Scotland"; but, when Boswell's business was over, they "parted quite placidly." So much so, in fact, that the younger man decided that he would "spare Hawkins as much as I in justice could" when he returned to his manuscript of the *Life of Samuel Johnson*.[28] We shall see how well he spared him.

III Miscellaneous Writings Between the Tour and the Life

Neither the quality nor the quantity of Boswell's writings between publication of the *Tour* and that of the *Life* warrants more than a passing mention. Recalling his zealous endeavors in behalf of the Scottish people before he had established himself in London, we see him sending to *Scots Magazine* another letter addressed to "the People of Scotland" urging them to petition for the restoration of juries in civil cases.[29] To *Gentleman's Magazine* he submitted a rambling review of John Gillies's *History of Greece*,[30] revealing his own enduring fascination for travel and for learning. Although a quarter of a century had passed since his Corsica days, he still had an interest in that country and its hero. In 1790 he sent a letter to *Scots Magazine* enclosing General Paoli's speech to the General Assembly of Corsica, which he had made after he was restored to his post as general of the national troops and as president of the General Assembly.[31]

Boswell sent to the press at this time several specimens of his generally banal and inept humorous verse, among which were his lines[32] in retaliation for some uncomplimentary lines written by Soame Jenyns on Johnson's death and some doggerel verse addressed to Charles Dilly,[33] which carries reference to convivial get-togethers with Dilly, Lettsom, and other gay friends. His "Epigram on the pusillanimous conduct of the French Troops against the Austrians at Tournay"[34] shows Boswell's strong opposition to the French Revolution. Formerly, when the Frenchmen were fighting for their king, they were brave; now "A strange reverse the Democrats display,/ And prove the Right of Man—to *run away*."

Another situation in international affairs prompted Boswell to bring forth another of his occasional absurdities: the success of Pitt's government in forestalling war with Spain by negotiating for trade privileges off the northwest coast of America. When Pitt's victory was announced at a great celebration in Guildhall on Lord Mayor's

Day in 1790, Boswell was on hand with a metrical broadside in praise of Pitt: *William Pitt, the Grocer of London*. Singing it before the assembled dignitaries, and thus making a spectacle of himself, he managed to extract only a forced smile from the prime minister, whose patronage he had intermittently attempted to secure and who henceforth had still better reasons for ignoring him.

We recall the clever journalism by which Boswell stirred up interest in the Corsican campaign for freedom and at the same time earned advance publicity for his book on that country. Another trick of his, apparently designed to promote his forthcoming *Life of Samuel Johnson*, was to advertise obscurely two extracts from the book before its publication so that the newspapers would be taken in and publish them, only to have to print apologies later, thus affording good publicity for the biography.[35] The extracts in question were calculated to catch the public fancy: *A Conversation between His Most Sacred Majesty George III and Samuel Johnson, LL.D.* and *The Celebrated Letter from Samuel Johnson, LL.D., to Philip Dormer Stanhope, Earl of Chesterfield.*

Nothing that the biographer wrote during the last ten years of his life, except the *Tour* and the *Life*, received so much notice from Boswell himself as his poem of 198 octosyllabic lines entitled *No Abolition of Slavery, or the Universal Empire of Love* (1791), which is a ridiculously incongruous tribute to lust and an attack on Wilberforce's bill for the abolition of the slave trade. His sentiments were expressed both in the text and in the rather copious notes accompanying it. Wilberforce's bill, if passed, would be a violation of the property rights of slaveowners and a disadvantage to the slaves themselves, he contended, in that it would "preclude them from the first step toward progressive civilization." He then asserted that, if slavery had disadvantages to those who were affected by it, those disadvantages would have to be taken as an evil which must of necessity accompany that foundation stone of society, subordination:

> From wise subordination's plan
> Springs the chief happiness of man;
> Yet from that source to numbers flow
> Varieties of pain and woe . . .

Nor must the zealous abolitionist deprive the planter of the licentious delights which he had a right to expect from the more shapely of his female slaves. The institution of slavery, Boswell continued, is ordained by God, as witness the Old and New Testaments. Furthermore, the slaves are happy as they sing at their work and look forward to the end of the day when they will eat good food and wear good clothes and enjoy their *amours* amid clean and pleasant surroundings.

The baseness of this argument may find some extenuation in the relative unpopularity of the movement to destroy the lucrative commerce in slaves, but what can account for the inferiority of this verse from the pen of the great biographer at the height of his career? We are forced to dismiss the publication of *No Abolition of Slavery* as one more of Boswell's incredible performances.

Not long before the appearance of Johnson's biography, Boswell's wife, finding the climate of London and other attending ills too great to bear, returned to Scotland where she hoped to regain her health. Meanwhile, her husband remained in the British capital, refusing to give up the idea of entering Parliament until the earl of Lonsdale, a powerful controller of electoral votes, led him on to bright political expectations and then brutally dropped him a few months before the *Life* came from the press. Micawber like, Boswell was always expecting something to turn up—something from the great magic hat of London.

Whatever his failures, whatever his deep disappointments, Boswell knew he had achieved. His Hebrides *Tour* had brought him solid recognition, though it was late in arriving. At any rate, he would have his portrait done by the most distinguished artist of the day; and what is more, he would write his memoirs. When Boswell did write them in his fifty-first year, he published them in *The European Magazine*[36] anonymously and in the third person; for, in so doing, he would seem to be getting deserved recognition. This short sketch, *Memoirs of James Boswell, Esq.* (1791), running in two installments, is a fairly straightforward account of his life which makes brief mention of his major works and of a very few minor ones.

This work is uncommonly significant in its incontestable proof that there had been no important change in Boswell through the years and that his view of himself had not changed. When he was a very young man, he enjoyed thinking of himself as a poet; he still did. Then he wanted to imagine he was a patron of literature; in retrospect, he said he had been just that. Then he was ostentatious and self-applauding; later he seemed delighted to say he had always been so; but, he added (and this is crucial!), his display of egotism had been "it would seem with a conscious smile."

Thus Boswell let the secret out. Thus he revealed a major technique used throughout the body of his works: the manipulation of himself as of a fictional character and the deliberate, sometimes stubbornly persistent, assumption of the image that he wished to see and that he wished others to see. Though not always obtrusive (and generally subdued), this assumed character pervaded his re-creation of Johnson's world in *The Life of Johnson*.

It is fortunate for students of Boswell that, during the early part of 1790 and the first few weeks of 1791 (until, in fact, shortly before the *Life* came off the press), Malone sojourned in Ireland, occasioning letters from Boswell that contain more information about his biographical labors than will be found elsewhere among his writings. There are nine letters from Boswell to Malone at this time, the first dated December 4, 1790, and the last March 8, 1791.[37] Aside from many other valuable bits of information, we learn that Boswell had received an account of Johnson from Johnson's friend Bennet Langton and several of his letters; that, because of a shortage of paper, his work met with delay; that he was tempted to accept a thousand pounds for his book because George Steevens, contending that curiosity about Johnson was confined to their small circle, advised him not to overprint; that the painter Sir Joshua Reynolds, not sharing Steevens's pessimism, voiced more sanguine hopes that were later to find ample justification; and that he had not yet prepared an account of Johnson's death.

CHAPTER 6

The Life of Samuel Johnson, LL.D

BOSWELL'S biography of Johnson treats his subject's conversation and the principal events of his life from day to day and from year to year from 1709 to 1784. Beyond this simple chronological arrangement of materials, there is no organization, no grouping of events into periods or phases of Johnson's life. Since the chief emphasis of the book is Johnson's talk from his fifty-fourth year, when he met his biographer, that portion of the work dealing with his life up to this year automatically falls into a division which is unique in that it does not have a single sustained conversation. The rest of the book can perhaps best be examined by viewing Boswell's account of the remaining twenty-one years of the already famous Johnson's life, which falls into two nearly even periods: one that saw the founding of the Literary Club and the publication of the Shakespeare edition; the other, his finest literary contribution—*The Lives of the English Poets.*

Boswell devoted the first few pages of the biography to an introduction in which he discussed his peculiar fitness for the great undertaking, his biographical method, and the inadequacies of Sir John Hawkins's biography of Johnson, which had recently been published.[1] He apologized for his presumption in attempting the life of the best biographer ever known. Referring to Johnson's statement in one of his essays to the effect that a man's life may best be written by himself, he declared that, had Johnson written his own life, he would have given to the world "the most perfect example of biography that was ever exhibited."[2] But Boswell left no doubt that he was eminently qualified to write this biography. He referred to his peculiar ability to remember Johnson's conversation and to his industry in recording it; and he stated that, during the twenty years that he had known him, Johnson had from time to time furnished him with materials on his early life. Moreover, Boswell had confidence in the superiority of his biographical method, which he explained in some detail.

In the first place, he would not melt down his materials "into one mass"; that is, he would not narrate except when necessary to "explain, correct, and supply." He would, rather, trace Johnson's life from year to year through conversation, letters, and other personal documents in order to furnish a more lively, lifelike, and complete picture of him. He then stated, in fact, that the unique characteristic of the work was the great quantity of instructive and entertaining conversation, to which he attributed the public's warm reception of his *Tour to the Hebrides;* and he cited Johnson himself and Plutarch, "the prince of ancient biographers," to the effect that the sayings and insignificant actions of a man, more than his great achievements, reveal his vices and virtues. Through the use of this method Johnson "would be preserved more completely in this work than any man who ever lived." He would not write a panegyric but take into account, as Johnson had for the subjects of his biographies, the blemishes as well as the ornaments. However tempted he might be to hide his friend's faults, his greater obligation was to knowledge and truth.

Sir John Hawkins's biography was the longest and most important of the lives of Johnson that came from the press after Boswell announced plans for publication of his own. Although Hawkins was the author of a valuable history of music, an original member of the famous Literary Club, and one of three executors of Johnson's estate, Boswell challenged his qualifications to write Johnson's life. He claimed that he had not seen Hawkins in Johnson's presence more than once; that he was too rigidly formal to have a companionable relationship with Johnson; and that he lacked the keen, sensitive perception necessary for discerning anything but the exterior of Johnson's makeup. Boswell thought that Hawkins might have made better use of the fragments of Johnson's diary to which he had had access as one of his executors. He admitted that some of the book's literary gossip was interesting; but, since only a small and inaccurate portion was devoted to Johnson, it remained, therefore, a hodgepodge of literary gossip and of lengthy extraneous passages from various works. Boswell declared that the many misrepresentations to Johnson's discredit in Hawkins's book gave it "a dark, uncharitable cast," and he all but established vindication from these misrepresentations as a major purpose of the *Life.*

I   To Johnson's Fifty-fourth Year

Boswell selected facts and incidents from Johnson's early life which he thought were formative of the Johnson that he had come to know. Born in Lichfield in 1709, he had inherited a strong body, a penchant for gloominess, and high church, royalist sentiments from his father Michael, a bookseller and stationer originally from Derbyshire, who was registered in St. Mary's Church as a "gentleman"—a term, Boswell was careful to point out, that no longer indicated gentility. He attributed Johnson's sound sense and piety to his mother's having come from sturdy yeoman stock. His precocious feat of committing to memory a collect from *The Book of Common Prayer* after having read it hardly more than twice foreshadowed the prodigious memory of his later years. His ambition to excel, and the added stimulation from the whip of his headmaster at the Lichfield School, made possible a good foundation in Latin during these early years, despite his indolence and near blindness in one eye. Early indications of a superior mind were also seen in his having been chosen to teach the younger boys in his next school, Stourbridge; in his competence as a poet before he was twenty years old; and in his having read so much before entering Oxford University that Dr. Adams, Headmaster of Pembroke College, claimed that he was better qualified than any other student who ever attended Pembroke.

Boswell also focused on a mind in the making as he related Johnson's Oxford experience. Arriving at the university in 1728 as a commoner on the strength of a well-to-do friend's promise to support him, Johnson soon made a name for himself throughout the university by rapidly and skillfully translating Pope's *Messiah* into Latin. He often had around him a group of young students reveling in his brilliant display of wit and in his habitual rebellion against authority. His rugged mind survived a strong attack of hypochondria, which he suffered during a vacation and from which he never fully recovered, leaving him in fear of insanity throughout his life. He was unable to remain at Oxford longer than three years, for his friend failed to provide the promised assistance. Preparing the reader for Johnson's frequent jaunts to Oxford in later years, Boswell pointed out his abiding love for Pembroke College, Oxford University, and his deep pride in its distinguished graduates. Johnson left Oxford in 1731 without a degree, regretting that Dr. Adams became his tutor only toward the close of his stay there.

Boswell next presented Johnson's varied experiences from the year he left Oxford, also the year of his father's death, until his departure for London six years later. In nearby Market-Bosworth, Johnson had made a try at teaching Latin to boys who hated it hardly less than he did his miserable existence as a kind of domestic chaplain in the home of one of the school's patrons. He soon went to Birmingham, where he lived for several months with his schoolmate, Edmund Hector. There he wrote his first periodical essays for a local newspaper, translated Lobo's *A Voyage to Abyssinia* (only the preface of which Boswell thought was written in Johnson's perspicuous and forceful style), and met and married Mrs. Elizabeth Porter, who was almost twice his age. He taught school near Lichfield, which consisted of David Garrick, the future famous actor, and only one other pupil. This venture, proving too dull, lasted only a year and a half, during which Johnson read and worked on his tragedy *Irene*.

Boswell collected a few salient and quaint details about Johnson and his wife. He learned from Garrick that Mrs. Johnson's appearance and manner were not inviting, although she seemed to inspire Johnson "with more than ordinary passion." Johnson's own appearance at the time was forbidding enough. With his hair straight and stiff and parted behind, he was big-boned and unwieldy in size, carried large scars from scrofula, and was given to rather frightening motions, which strongly resembled convulsive gesticulations of one hand and one leg. We see this odd couple on their wedding morning traveling three miles on horseback to church. She complained that he was riding too fast; but, to show who was master from the start, he quickened his pace and passed her. When she caught up with him, she was in tears. But he was affectionate to his Tetty (or Tetsy, as he sometimes called her) for the rest of his life. He told a mutual friend of his and Boswell's that it was on both sides a love marriage. There is little about her in the *Life*. When she died, after spending all but three of her seventeen years as Mrs. Johnson with her husband in London, Johnson's Negro servant Francis Barber witnessed deep suffering on Johnson's part, which he later reported to Boswell.

When Johnson was twenty-eight years old, he went to London; he was accompanied by his former pupil David Garrick, who, soon becoming the greatest actor of his age, preceded his master in the enjoyment of London's acclaim. During his first months in the capital, Johnson experienced disappointment and privation; but he obtained some financial relief from writing for Edward Cave's highly regarded *Gentleman's Magazine*, to which he contributed for many years. He eked out a bare subsistence from editing, translating, and reporting parliamentary debates under the title of "The Senate of Lilliput," and he tried unsuccessfully to produce the declamatory tragedy *Irene*.

Boswell's method was to list Johnson's works for each year, beginning with 1738, his first year in London, and to present facts of publication and literary history, along with brief or lengthy criticisms of some of the works. *London*, Johnson's first successful poem, was published in this year. As Boswell compared it with a poetical satire on London by John Oldham, his critical comments on the poem, as on most of Johnson's works, were sensible and judicious. Alexander Pope, having read the poem and knowing nothing of the author except it, praised Johnson to a friend, who in turn wrote to Dean Jonathan Swift of Trinity College, Dublin, asking Swift to use his good services in procuring for Johnson a master's degree. This recommendation, explained Boswell, was for the purpose of helping the poverty-stricken Johnson become eligible for the headmastership of a school; but nothing came of it.

Boswell devoted considerable space to Johnson's next work, a biography of Richard Savage, published in 1744. During Johnson's early years in London, he and Savage, a profligate poet with an engaging personality, struck up a strong friendship; both, totally broke and unable to pay for lodgings, sometimes roamed the streets all night. In keeping with Boswell's aim not to write a panegyric but to present the true Johnson, he took the opportunity, as he discussed this book, to suggest that Johnson hardly adhered to his principles of good conduct during these years when he and Savage fraternized together and that his indulgences led to "much distress of his virtuous mind." Boswell praised the book for its authenticity and its entertaining and vigorous style, but he was less concerned with a criticism of it than with what the book revealed of Johnson's prejudices against actors, and with the controversy regarding whether Savage was, as he claimed to be, the illegitimate son of the countess of Macclesfield, whose atrocities against him were minutely detailed in Johnson's biography. Boswell included too much of his own argument to show that Savage was an impostor.

In much of the section of the *Life* now under consideration, Boswell concentrated more on literary history relating to Johnson than on his personal life; and this observation is particularly true of treatment of the remaining 1740's. The public rejected Garrick's production of Johnson's twice revised *Irene*, which Boswell thought worthy as a poem but poor as a tragedy because of its deficiency in pathos; but the poem *Vanity of Human Wishes*, with its impressive philosophic dignity, was well received despite its insufficient realism. Johnson was preparing an edition of Shakespeare; sending translations and other items to *Gentleman's Magazine*, including some verses which in Boswell's estimation were merely "namby-pamby rhymes"; and making preliminary preparations for compiling a dictionary. Boswell wrote an engaging account of the methods that Johnson and his amanuenses used in the making of the dictionary in the upper room of his Gough Street lodgings. He would mark with a heavy black pencil passages in various books that were to be used in etymologies and definitions. Five of his six amanuenses, Boswell was proud to report, were Scotsmen. With this small staff of workers Johnson intended to complete the dictionary in about three years—it actually required over seven—while it took the forty members of the French Academy forty years to complete their dictionary.

Boswell placed much stress on Johnson's role as a teacher of religious and moral wisdom, his chief vehicle of instruction being *The Rambler*, which, except for a few single contributions of different persons, was composed of weekly papers by Johnson that ran for two years beginning in March, 1750. Boswell's critical remarks on the six volumes of these essays were careful and thorough. He attributed the unpopularity of the essays to their solemnity and single authorship, and he praised the vigor and perspicuity of the writing, admitting that Johnson was addicted to Latinized expansions and inversions and to philosophical terms to express simple ideas. Boswell revealed his competence in the history of English prose styles as he pointed out the influence on Johnson of Richard Hooker, Sir Francis Bacon, Sir Thomas Browne, and others. Addison, he thought, wrote with the ease of a gentleman; Johnson, like a teacher dictating "from his academical chair."

In light but telling strokes Boswell described the griefstricken Johnson on the occasion of his wife's death in 1752, and he refuted Hawkins's charge that Johnson dissembled his love for her. The account of Johnson's life from this point to the publication of his dictionary in 1755 includes his occasional papers for *The Adventurer*, a trip to Oxford for library research in connection with his dictionary, the receiving of a master of arts degree from Oxford University on the basis of the influence of his essays on religion and morals and the power of their language, his great plans for the dictionary, and a letter to Lord Chesterfield regarding them.

When Johnson published his *Plan* for the dictionary, he inscribed it to Lord Chesterfield because of the interest he had shown in the ambitious project, but in subsequent years, when he tried more than once to solicit his attention, Chesterfield ignored him. Finally, when the great book was well underway and Chesterfield deigned to write complimentary expressions in *The World,* Johnson wrote him a letter that has resounded through the years as heralding the independence from patronage of the profession of letters. Published in Johnson's own day, it was then famous and remains so. He told Chesterfield in dignified but sharp terms that, having been repulsed at his door for seven years, he could complete the project without his assistance.

Commenting critically on the dictionary, which was published in 1755, Boswell noticed Johnson's clear expression of abstract scientific ideas; his extensive reading, as reflected in his accumulation of authorities; and his intellectual acuteness. He pointed out that there were, to be sure, some wrong definitions. When a lady asked Johnson why he defined *pastern* as the knee of a horse and expected him to defend the definition, he suprisingly answered, "Ignorance, Madam, pure ignorance." Some definitions, Boswell explained, employ words that are more difficult than the terms defined—like, for instance, "desiccative" for *dry*. Others are humorous, like "a harmless drudge" for *a lexicographer*. Johnson received only 1570 pounds for the work; and, after paying his helpers, he had only a pittance left for himself.

Boswell next called attention to Johnson's periodical paper the *Idler* and to his didactic romance, *Rasselas*. Many of the *Idler* essays, he pointed out, were dashed off hurriedly and have "less body" but are more lively and have "a greater facility of language" than the *Rambler* papers. He thought highly of Johnson's philosophical novel *Rasselas*, which he wrote in the evenings of one week in order to defray the expenses for the funeral of his mother, who died in his fiftieth year. This work alone, wrote Boswell, was enough to insure Johnson's immortality; yet he received only a hundred

pounds for the first edition and twenty-five for the second. Translated into most modern languages and distributed all over Europe,
it treated, as did Voltaire's *Candide*, the theme of more evil than
good in this life; but, unlike *Candide*, which ridiculed religion, as
Boswell pointed out, *Rasselas* turned men's minds against the
unsatisfactory nature of the temporal life and directed them to hope
for things eternal.

Johnson's kindness of heart and his benevolent treatment of the
unfortunate are seen in the odd assortment of the souls who found
refuge in his household. There was Robert Levet, grotesque, formal,
and silent, who practiced medicine of a sort only among poor
people. For many years he stayed with Johnson and waited on him
like a servant, Johnson all the while generally preferring him to
regular physicians. Mrs. Anna Williams, the blind daughter of a
physician, came to Johnson's house by way of Mrs. Johnson. She
lived there nearly twenty years and had a strong influence on
Johnson. Anyone whom Johnson invited to have tea with him and
Mrs. Williams could well consider himself highly favored. Goldsmith and Boswell vied with each other for the honor. Two of the
persons in the house were out-and-out charity cases: Miss Car-
michael ("Poll") and Mrs. Desmoulins. There was little peace
among the group, as Johnson indicated in a letter to a friend:
"Mrs. Williams hates everybody, Levett hates Desmoulins, and
does not love Williams; Desmoulins hates them both; Poll loves
none of them." Johnson's Negro servant, Francis Barber, who also
lived in the house, came from the West Indies. He had been freed
by his master and turned over to Johnson. Shortly before his death,
more than thirty years after Barber came on the scene, Johnson
willed him most of his money and belongings. A later but by no
means insignificant member of the household was Hodge the cat,
for whom his fond master would go out to buy oysters.

By the late 1750's some of Johnson's circle of distinguished
associates and friends had already appeared on the scene: Sir
Joshua Reynolds, the great painter and actual founder of the Literary Club; the actor David Garrick; William Strahan, Scots printer
living in London, who accepted Gibbon's *Decline and Fall of the
Roman Empire* after it had been turned down by several other
printers; Bennet Langton, tall and lean Greek scholar, many of
whose letters provided important information for the *Life;* and
Topman Beauclerk, the witty, malicious, merry, excellent conver-

sationalist, lover of learning, and collector of rare books. After he and Langton had sat in a tavern until three o'clock one morning, they thought they would knock on Johnson's door and rouse him for a ramble for the rest of the night. Since he was quite ready to comply, they walked to a tavern, drank a bowl of "bishop," took a boat down the Thames, and spent the remainder of the day in pleasant dissipation. This and certain other incidents related by Boswell belie the charge sometimes made that Boswell gave us only the stern side of Johnson.

II *Johnson after Boswell—to 1775*

The relation of biographer to subject is intrinsic to the content, form, and texture of a biography. Whether they are separated by centuries or united by blood or ties of friendship, whether divided by clashing ideologies or drawn together by mutually compatible beliefs and outlooks, the nature of the biographer's concern with the truth of his subject, and indeed his vision of that truth, will be crucially affected. The significance of Johnson and Boswell's relationship unfolds as we become involved in Johnson's story. This relationship began one day in the spring of 1763, when Johnson walked into Davies's bookshop and into Boswell's life—and the twenty-two-year-old Boswell entered a life story that had been in progress for fifty-four years.

Granted a pension by the king the year before, Johnson's niche in England's Hall of Celebrities was now already secure. He was known for his essays, his dictionary, and his poetry; but his edition of Shakespeare and his *Lives of the English Poets* were yet to adorn that niche. The young Boswell, eager to be known as an author and a wit but perceptive enough to distinguish between cheap notoriety and fame arising out of solid achievement, had dabbled in poetry and essays and had practiced taking down conversation with a view to writing somebody's life story. He had come to the bookshop several times hoping to meet Johnson, who he heard often dropped by there to chat and browse. When Davies saw Johnson through the glass door, he announced his "aweful approach" in a manner that brought to Boswell's mind an actor's announcement of the Ghost's appearance in *Hamlet:* "Look, my Lord, it comes." Boswell emerges in his narration of this auspicious meeting as so awed by Johnson's presence that he fumbled and blundered, evoking from the great man a cutting remark about the Scots and a withering rebuff for speaking out of turn. But Boswell forthwith collected himself and made the most of this momentous hour, which he had anticipated for so long.

He listened attentively to Johnson's talk; and later during the day he recorded, as we are informed in a footnote, what he said of the private lives of authors, primitive living versus civilized society, an Englishman's notion of liberty, Thomas Sheridan (father of Richard Brinsley Sheridan, the dramatist), and other subjects. Boswell was pleased with the "extraordinary vigour" of Johnson's conversation; and he concluded that, despite "the roughness in his manner, there was no ill-nature in his disposition." Boswell's resolution and common sense stood him in good stead, for eight days later one of the world's most celebrated literary friendships was sealed when Johnson, dressed in loose britches and unbuckled shoes and wearing an unpowdered wig, warmly received the persevering young Scotsman in his Inner Temple chambers.

Boswell properly faded into the background; and, except for a few times when he intruded brazenly and without apparent justification, he kept the focus on Johnson. When he recorded his talk and what he saw and heard of him from May 16 until August 6, the day he left London, he was doing so for his private Journal and not for the *Life;* for he had not yet decided to write it. There is nothing in his method of reporting to suggest that he went about with notebook in hand taking down Johnson's every word. In fact, Boswell now and then so completely surrendered himself to Johnson's conversation that he forgot he wanted to record it later. But he worked hard at his task of keeping a full journal, relishing it as an art to be perfected. In fact, when he began to write the *Life,* he actually referred in its pages to his method of preserving Johnson's talk, which he said was imperfect during those first few weeks of their acquaintance; for he had not yet become "strongly impregnated with the.Johnsonian aether." He soon became so impregnated, however; and, when he took the trouble, he could even transform into Johnson's best style conversation reported to him.[3]

The distinguished men and women with whom Johnson was on intimate terms, often referred to as "Johnson's circle" (and at least once by Boswell as "the Johnsonian school"), constitute one of the book's chief sources of delight. The nucleus of this company was that group of men whose achievements in literature, science, politics, religion, and the arts rendered it one of the most select groups in history. First proposed by Sir Joshua Reynolds and known as "the Literary Club," or just "the Club," it existed before it was formally instituted in 1764; and, from its beginning until his death, Johnson dominated it with his brilliant talk and commanding personality. The men gathered once each week at the Turk's Head, but occasionally they changed the day and place of meeting. After dining, they talked until late in the evening.

The original members were, beside Reynolds and Johnson, Edmund Burke, Oliver Goldsmith, Sir John Hawkins, Dr. Christopher Nugent, Burke's Roman Catholic father-in-law, who moved to London from Ireland, Beauclerk, Langton, and the wealthy and liberally educated gentleman stockbroker Andrew Chamier. Later members were Edward Gibbon, who was blackballed on the first try; the Shakespearean editors Edmund Malone and George Steevens; the antiquarian Bishop Thomas Percy; the historian and economist Adam Smith; the actor David Garrick; the politician and member of Parliament John Courtenay; the dramatist Richard Brinsley Sheridan; and Boswell, who was elected to membership ten years after he met Johnson.

Johnson's circle, as it extended beyond the Club, encompassed, among others, General Paoli (during his exile in London); General Oglethorpe, former governor and virtual founder of Georgia, who returned to London and resumed a parliamentary career begun in earlier years; and the wealthy Henry Thrale and his wife Hester, whose grand residence was the scene of many a splendid gathering of wits and people of rank. Johnson, as we have already indicated, formed a close personal relationship with the Thrales; and they extended him living quarters, which he occupied for a number of years as one of the family. He also saw much of Miss Frances Burney, author of the novel *Evelina* and she recorded some valuable anecdotes about him in her *Diary;*[4] but, except for a tea at which she was in Johnson's presence, and to which Boswell spared only three lines, there are no other scenes involving her in the *Life*— only an occasional mention of her.

A fitting designation of Johnson's sociability, which found its best expression in club gatherings, is an apt coinage that he applied in compliment to Boswell: *Clubbable*. He himself was one of the most clubbable of men. During those early years in London, while he was working on the dictionary, he formed the Ivy Lane Club;

and, in his seventy-fourth year, he founded the Essex Head Club. Members in these clubs were not particularly noteworthy, if we except Dr. Richard Bathurst (in the first) and Dr. Richard Brocklesby (in the second), the close friend of Edward Burke and the attendant on Johnson during his dying hours.

After the biographer had caught up with Johnson's life to the point where he could give fresh, firsthand accounts of various events, the movement became slower, allowing for more vivid closeups of assemblies of distinguished persons. One such assembly that took place in Sir Joshua Reynolds's spacious home was particularly memorable. Quite a large gathering was there to hear Dr. Johnson tell about a chance interview with the king. He held them in rapt attention as he told the story, which Boswell later published separately. On one of his visits to the queen's library adjoining the Palace, the librarian, as he had been ordered to do beforehand, quietly stole out of the library and fetched the king, who talked with Johnson at length about literature. He revealed a considerable knowledge of it, not excluding some of Johnson's own writings, on which His Majesty was pleased to compliment him. When he suggested that Johnson write the literary history of his country, he graciously indicated his willingness to comply. With customary skill, Boswell grasped the drama of the occasion at Sir Joshua's. At first Johnson felt indisposed to talk about this experience, but he was soon prevailed upon to do so. As his friends gathered around and listened attentively, Goldsmith, seated on a sofa at some distance, appeared singularly uninterested and unmoved, as if with envy; but he suddenly reached forward and shook Johnson's hand, admitting that, had he been in Johnson's place, he would probably have have "bowed and stammered through the whole of it."

Goldsmith, whom Boswell described as "one of the brightest ornaments of the Johnsonian school," was the son of an Irish clergyman. Educated at Trinity College, Dublin, he applied for ordination but was rejected. He next studied medicine, moved to London, and practiced in nearby Southwark. When he met Johnson in 1761, he was barely making ends meet from his meager practice and from what he could earn as a hack writer. By the time he joined the Club as an original member three years later, he was coming into prominence as a writer, having published *Enquiry into the Present State of Polite Learning, Citizen of the World*, and other works.

He had written, but not published, *The Vicar of Wakefield.*

Boswell devoted much space to Goldsmith as a leading character in Johnson's story, but the image that emerges is anything but attractive. He is represented as always too eager to "shine" in conversation; but, except for occasional flashes of wit, his efforts were miserable failures. Habitual envy and jealousy accentuated the coarseness of his outward appearance. Respectfully attached to Johnson at first, he later allowed his literary successes to create in him the vain desire to compete. He lied when he said he received four hundred pounds for *The Vicar of Wakefield,* for Johnson took the manuscript to the bookseller and sold it for sixty pounds in order to free Goldsmith from arrest for debt by his landlady.

It could be argued that Boswell was retaliating with this unpleasant image of Goldsmith because of his ambitions and successes. Whatever the case, he presented expressions by Johnson and others of high praise for Goldsmith's works, he gave due recognition to what he thought was his tender and generous heart, and he was deeply affected when Goldsmith's death ten years before Johnson's removed him from the circle where he well belonged but in which he fitted so awkwardly. Boswell's report of an incident involving a memorial for Goldsmith suggests the solid esteem in which he was held by his fellows and at the same time reflects upon their awesome regard for Johnson and their unwillingness to cross him.

When Goldsmith died, Johnson, at the request of members of the Club, wrote a Latin epitaph for Goldsmith's monument in Westminster Abbey. After the first version was submitted to the members for their criticism, they wrote down suggestions for revision, one of which was that the epitaph be written in English; but, since no one had the courage to sign his name first, they decided upon the famous Round Robin, which was the writing of their signatures so as to form a circle and thus conceal the identity of the first signer. When Reynolds presented the paper to Johnson, he responded with good humor; but he said "*he would never consent to disgrace the walls of Westminster Abbey with an English inscription.*"

Of the many great men who are alive in this book, several deserve special mention: Edmund Burke, Sir Joshua Reynolds, Edward Gibbon, Adam Smith, and David Garrick. Burke was best known as a distinguished Whig politician, whose speeches in Parliament and whose writings in opposition to the conduct of the war against the

Americans and to the principles of the French Revolution made him famous. During the 1760's and earlier 1770's, the period of Johnson's life now under consideration, Burke was already known as the author of *A Vindication of Natural Society and A Philosophical Inquiry into the Sublime and Beautiful*. Boswell represented him as especially respectful to Johnson, whose pension he defended when it came up in Parliament, although they differed politically. Johnson remarked that Burke, like all Whigs, was "a cursed Whig"; revered him nevertheless; and regretted that his speeches against the Stamp Act so raised him in the public eye that he became too busy to attend meetings of the Club.

Burke was, in fact, the only member whose wit was a challenge to Johnson. Once, when Johnson was unable to exert himself because of illness, he said, Burke's name having been mentioned, "That fellow calls forth all my powers. Were I to see Burke now, it would kill me." Boswell attributed this remark to Johnson's notion of conversation as a contest and to his estimate of Burke as an opponent. "It is very pleasing to me to record, that Johnson's high estimation of the talents of this gentleman was uniform from their early acquaintance."

Sir Joshua Reynolds, one of the greatest portrait painters of history, was the first president of the Royal Academy of Arts; but his fifteen *Discourses* on painting and the principles of art, because of their literary merit, entitle him to a place among men of letters. Goldsmith dedicated his *Deserted Village* to him and Boswell his *Life of Samuel Johnson*, in which Reynolds plays one of the leading roles. He did portraits of nearly all the socialites and persons of rank in the England of his day, and his home was the scene of many a brilliant gathering of wits and celebrities. Boswell, in his dedication to Reynolds, quoted Johnson as saying that he was "the most venerable man" he knew. Reynolds admired Johnson's "accuracy and flow of language," but he stood his ground in an argument with him concerning the power of moderate drinking as a mental enlivener. Once Johnson refused to argue with him on the subject, for Reynolds had been drinking and had reached the stage where he "mistook words for thoughts."

Edward Gibbon, who spent twenty years of his life doing research for and writing his celebrated *Decline and Fall of the Roman Empire*, succeeded Goldsmith as Professor in Ancient History in the Royal Academy of Arts. It is fairly certain that he was blackballed when first presented for membership in the Club, and his lack of rapport with Johnson's group is suggested by the very few times that he appeared at meetings of the Club or at other gatherings. Boswell, who admired. David Hume in spite of his atheism. contemptuously referred to Gibbon as an infidel nearly every one of the few times he mentioned him in the *Life*; for he objected to the uncandid and oblique way that Gibbon in the *Decline* had supported atheism.[5] Although Gibbon was a member of the Club during the approximately ten years when Johnson presided over it (in fact, even until ten years after Johnson's death), he appeared in the *Life* very few times, either directly or indirectly as a subject of conversation.

Another member of Johnson's circle to produce one of the world's celebrated books was Adam Smith, whose *Wealth of Nations* was a revolutionary classic in economic theory. When he was Professor of Logic at Glasgow University, he formed a friendship with the philosopher David Hume and later edited his autobiography. Three years before Smith's death in 1790, he became Rector of Glasgow University. He lived in London off and on while working on his magnum opus, but he does not seem to have spent much time with fellow members of the Club. According to Boswell, his conversational powers were not highly esteemed; his mind was crowded with a variety of subjects, but he lacked Johnson's "force, acuteness, and vivacity," and he generally spoke in a "decisive professorial manner."

When Smith's qualifications for writing *The Wealth of Nations* were questioned because of his not having engaged in trade, Johnson defended him; but he is reported not to have taken to Smith until he learned of his preference for rhyme over blank verse. During Boswell's short stay at Glasgow, when he took Smith's lectures on rhetoric, he was well pleased with him, but he had become disenchanted with him by the time he began work on the manuscript for the *Life*. Boswell objected to the wholesale attacks, rather than those on "certain particulars," which Smith leveled on his own alma mater, Oxford University, as well as to his "ill-founded" and "invidious" charge that the English universities were too rich in financial resources for learning to flourish adequately.

Johnson's former pupil, David Garrick, arrived in London to study law; but his passion for the stage prevailed, and his per-

formance of the leading role in *Richard III* soon brought him fame
and fortune. As manager of Drury Lane Theatre, he tried in vain
to produce the struggling and impecunious Johnson's plodding
tragedy *Irene*. Johnson's already low estimate of the profession
of acting was not likely to lessen the indignation which he must
have felt on being, as Boswell put it, "outstripped by his pupil."
He took a dim view of Garrick's living "in more splendor than is
suitable for a player," and he was piqued on hearing that he was
unduly confident of being elected to the Club (of which, it might
be noted, he was not an original member). It appears, though, that
Johnson grew to appreciate Garrick's worth and felt that he had
"advanced the dignity of his profession." He was surprised, in
fact, that Garrick kept his head as well as he did, considering the
crowd's dinning applause each night; and, in view of his belonging
to a profession noted for its licentiousness, he admired him for
living decently, if splendidly. If his conversation lacked substance,
thought Johnson, it was at least "sprightly." Like Burke, Garrick
was too engaged to spend much time with Johnson's group; but
he is mentioned in the *Life*, or appears as a topic of conversation,
more often even than Burke.

Improvement in Johnson's personal circumstances as he
approached the last ten years of his life seemed to increase his
relish for London life and to whet his appetite for talk. Honored
with a doctor's degree from Dublin's Trinity College, he now
became "Dr. Johnson." With the publication of his edition of
Shakespeare, which Boswell commended for its eloquent language,
its recognition of Shakespeare's defects, and its restraint from the
usual uncritical praise that was characteristic of other Shakespearean commentators, all of Johnson's important works, except
The Lives of the English Poets, had already come from the press.
He took one of his most delightful trips to Oxford, from which
Boswell harvested a rich treasure of conversation on subjects ranging
from a play by Goldsmith and a comparative estimate of Fielding
and Richardson to adultery and a scorpion's behavior while in a
center of burning coals. When he went with Boswell into Scotland
and the Hebrides Islands, Johnson enjoyed the longest and most
enjoyable vacation of his life. Lasting a hundred days in the
summer and fall of 1773, it was recorded, as we have noted, in
published books by both travelers.[6] Boswell devoted only about a
page in the *Life* and an informative and entertaining footnote to it,

in which he explained why Johnson returned from Scotland convinced that, during his stay in Boswell's Edinburgh home, he had incurred Mrs. Boswell's eternal dislike: his hours were irregular and his habits uncouth. He had turned the candles downward to make them burn more briskly, letting wax drop on the carpet.

III *Johnson's Last Ten Years*

The portion of the *Life* dealing with Johnson's activities after he returned from Scotland is comprised mainly of many letters between him and his biographer concerning such subjects as the Club—who was accepted, who was rejected: the death of Goldsmith; and the state of the controversy between Johnson and the Scots poet James MacPherson, who had published supposed translations of ancient Scottish (Erse or Gaelic) poems, now known to be fabrications. MacPherson told Boswell he had offered originals of the third-century poet Ossian to Johnson so that, with the help of Gaelic readers, he could see that they were originals. When Johnson denied that MacPherson had made such an offer, MacPherson threatened him with physical violence. Boswell printed Johnson's letter to MacPherson (already published in newspapers) in which Johnson replied that "the menaces of a ruffian" were not enough to deter him from exposing what he considered a cheat. Delighted at Johnson's courage, Boswell reported other evidences of it—how, for instance, Johnson threw a man into the pit when he sat in his chair at the theater; separated two large fighting dogs; kept at bay four men who attacked him in the street; and directly swam into a pool after Langton cautioned him that it was dangerous to do so.

Boswell moved from the discussion of Johnson and MacPherson into a defense of Johnson against charges that he was excessively prejudiced against Scottish people and their country. Johnson recognized that it was a point of national pride for Scots to want to accept Ossian as genuine, but disbelief in its authenticity was confirmed during his journey by careful examination of the evidence. Boswell nevertheless allowed for some prejudice from Johnson, "the true-born Englishman"; but his was "a prejudice of the head and not of the heart." He held that Johnson carried no ill will against the Scots, and he quoted statements from several Scotsmen who praised him for his treatment of Scotland in the narrative of his Hebrides trip, *Journey to the Western Islands of Scotland.*

Boswell reported that Oxford University, in conferring the Doctor of Civil Laws degree upon Johnson, honored him not only for the elegance of the language of his essays but for his championing of the cause of religion and morality. Yet, curiously enough, *Taxation, No Tyranny*, which came off the press the same year that he received the Oxford degree (1775), showed such violent support of England's treatment of the Americans, Boswell declared, that he lacked "the mildness of a Christian philosopher." Writing no panegyric, Boswell often freely expressed his opposition to Johnson's views and sometimes to his actions.

Boswell's report of Johnson's two months' tour of France with the Thrales of necessity differs sharply in treatment from his accounts of Johnson's excursion into Scotland. In the first place, Boswell did not accompany him to France and had to rely on only a portion of Johnson's minutely detailed account of his trip. This portion had somehow become separated from the rest of the account, which was either lost among other notes and papers or burned just before Johnson's death—before Boswell got around to asking Johnson to let him see them. Also, it should be remembered, Johnson was away from his native England, from his beloved London. When Boswell said to him as they traveled in the Hebrides Islands that that was the first time Johnson had seen anything but his native island, Johnson answered, "But, Sir, by seeing London I have seen as much of life as the world can shew."[7]

France showed him little that pleased or excited him. Some Frenchmen, he noticed, lived magnificently; but there was no middle class as in England. The people were indelicate; they spit anywhere. With so many shops open, Sunday seemed like any other day. Magnificent homes and churches were so common that if a man saw one, he had seen them all. Johnson disliked the food and thought the market meats were fit only to be used in England's jails. He had, however, a good word to say for the French beds; and, when he went to the court and was close enough to the king to see him eat, he was pleased to find him using his left hand just as they did in England.

Boswell stated several times that Johnson's talk was the chief thing in the *Life*. Even his literary career is of secondary importance, for we have to look elsewhere for a fuller and more conveniently presented history of it. But the talk is not all that is best conveyed by Boswell. We have, for example, the quietly human experiences of Johnson as he made the rounds of old acquaintances on his jaunts to neighboring places outside London, like the one to Oxford, Stratford-on-Avon, Birmingham, Lichfield, and Ashbourne. We find him at Oxford's Pembroke College walking in the master's garden with his old teacher Dr. Adams and recalling that there he used to play drafts with Phil Jones, who was fond of beer and later failed in the church, and with one Fluyder, who turned out to be a Whig scoundrel. We see Johnson at the Three Crowns Inn in Lichfield next door to where he was born, dining with an old school fellow and patiently listening to him explain his scheme of dressing leather; sitting in the pit of the theater and "receiving affectionate homage" from his friends and acquaintances; enjoying the pleasant garden, spacious home, and good table of his boyhood friend and school fellow, the Reverend John Taylor in Ashbourne. In intimate situations like these we glimpse the warmth and essential humanity in Johnson's makeup. His compassionate concern for his fellows, another trait revealed in the biography, is strongly evident in his involvement in the unfortunate affairs of the Reverend William Dodd.

Dodd, a clergyman of parts, well trained and effective in the pulpit, allowed his popularity to overthrow him. Extravagant living required more money than he was earning. After forging Lord Chesterfield's name to a bond, he was imprisoned, tried, and sentenced to death. Thousands of letters poured in to the king asking that he withdraw the death sentence, and Johnson was a persistent campaigner for a stay of his execution. Boswell listed Johnson's works in behalf of the unhappy clergyman, which he said were later published by ten booksellers of London in their edition of Johnson's works: Dodd's speech to the Recorder of London when sentence was about to be pronounced, his "Address to His Unhappy Brethren" (a sermon which he delivered in the chapel at Newgate), letters to Lord Mansfield and Lord Chancellor Bathurst, a petition of Mrs. Dodd to the queen, and Dr. Dodd's last solemn declaration, which Johnson left with the sheriff at the place of Dodd's execution. Boswell quoted from various *unpublished* letters relating to the case that Johnson wrote to Dodd and others. Johnson felt that Dodd's punishment was incommensurate with his wrongdoings, and his exertions for Dodd's reprieve take up many pages of the *Life*. His pleas for commiseration and for changing the penalty from death to exile went unheeded.

One of the amazing episodes in the story of Johnson—and here we must say Johnson and Boswell—was the clever arrangement by which Boswell brought together Johnson and the notorious politician John Wilkes, the Whiggest of Whigs, and therefore to Johnson a scoundrel among scoundrels. "Two men more different," wrote Boswell, "could perhaps not be selected out of all mankind." Wilkes had been expelled from the House of Commons and imprisoned in the Tower of London for a violent attack on the king and his minister Lord Bute. Popular with the crowd, he was three times reelected as a member from Middlesex and three times refused a seat. After he became lord mayor of London in 1774, he won a victory in the House of Commons, where the previous resolutions against him were nullified.

Boswell managed to bring his friends Edward and Charles Dilly, the booksellers, around to inviting Johnson and himself to a dinner at which Wilkes would also be present. He then maneuvered Johnson's consent to go to the Dillys', not by directly asking him to accept their invitation to dine, but by getting him to agree to go there and then insinuating that perhaps he would not be happy with the company. Johnson thereupon became indignant that his ability to adjust to Wilkes or any other company was thus being challenged. When the time came, he said that he had forgotten about it and blandly stated that he could not go because he was engaged to dine at home with the blind Mrs. Williams. Boswell then had to inveigle her into releasing Johnson from his engagement with her—a hard task. This accomplished and the two having arrived at the Dillys', he had to cope with Johnson's awkward behavior at the time of the sitting down at the table, but misgivings were short-lived.

Wilkes placed himself beside Johnson and was so exceedingly gracious in manner and so ready to talk about literature and other matters that Johnson was completely won over. His manner at first was polite, yet a bit surly; but he gradually became amiable and good humored; and he appeared thoroughly to enjoy his new friend. The affair lasted for hours, and Boswell reported one of the longest and most sparkling conversations in the *Life*. On subsequent occasions Johnson and Wilkes found pleasure in each other's company. Of Boswell's achievement, Burke remarked that "there was nothing to equal it in the whole history of the Corps Diplomatique."[8]

The biography conveys a sense of accelerated social and literary activity in Johnson's life toward the end of the 1770's that extended into the next decade. It might seem that he wished to avoid witnessing the wretchedness of those poor inmates who found protection under his roof from the insecurities of life. There was no end of breakfasts, teas, and dinners at Langton's, Beauclerk's, Oglethorpe's, Paoli's, Dilly's, Percy's, Reynolds's, the Thrales' and other homes, to say nothing of frequent get-togethers at taverns and coffeehouses. Conversation was ever the prime interest. Once at Reynolds's place each person presented at dinner recollected, various lines from Horace on Horace's Villa; and, after dinner, all retired to the drawing room, where they were joined by "a rich assembly," including Mrs. Hanna Moore, whose many tracts included a work on London society, of which she was a leading member.

Johnson was sometimes present at evening gatherings with Mrs. Moore and other clever and vivacious ladies. Such assemblies, where ladies gathered to converse with wits and men of letters, were known as Blue Stocking Clubs.[9] Langton sent Boswell an engaging account of one of these assemblies in the home of Mrs. Elizabeth Vesey, who was noted for her London parties. When Johnson entered, "the company began to collect around him, till they became not less than four, if not five deep; those behind standing, and listening over the heads of those that were sitting near him."

Boswell ably demonstrated his fitness for the task of writing a literary history of Johnson as he discussed Johnson's *Lives of the English Poets*, which was published in 1781 in Johnson's seventy-second year. He commented on Johnson's fullness of mind which qualified him for the undertaking. He explained that Johnson had intended merely prefaces but in every respect he had "produced an ample, rich, and most entertaining view" of the poets. Boswell described how Johnson in preparing the work went to various persons for quotations, anecdotes, items of literary history, and help in copying. He had asked for only two hundred pounds for the work, but was given a hundred pounds over that amount, still a meager reward for his achievement.

In discussing some of the lives separately, Boswell presented a few passages from each life that were revisions of earlier versions, concluding that the amendments were generally superior to the originals. He took special notice of Johnson's easy style and the sparsity of uncommon or learned words ("his legs grew tumic" for *his legs swelled*, for instance). In the Cowley life, where Johnson discussed the metaphysical poets, he discovered Dryden as "a new planet in the poetical hemisphere." While he attacked Milton's politics, he gave full credit to his poetic powers. His character of Dryden, Boswell stated, might have been Johnson's own: "strong reason" rather than "quick sensibility" was characteristic of his "intellectual operations"; and he "studied rather than felt." Boswell believed that Johnson's *Pope* was a labor of love; that it would have been better had Johnson refrained from giving the account of Addison's going to the law to collect a hundred pounds from Steele; and that Johnson did well to attack Swift for violating the precepts of subordination in affecting "familiarity with the great," which was a "transgression of regularity."

Not long after publication of the *Lives of the English Poets* (1781), the clouds began to collect over Johnson; and Boswell succeeded in conveying this effect. Johnson's health gradually failed: he suffered a severe stroke of palsy and temporarily lost his powers of speech, and he had a violent attack of asthma. When Levet died, there was no one left in the house but two old, sick women; and Mr. Thrale's death caused Johnson to spend less and less time at Streatham. Even before Mr. Thrale died, the relationship between Johnson and Mrs. Thrale had suffered a change. With her husband no longer curbing her lively inclinations and having had for a number of years enough of the great Johnson's society, she came gradually to lose her desire to please him, hardly keeping up even the appearance of friendship. Then, to Johnson's mortification she married a man of whom he strongly disapproved: Signor Piozzi, an Italian music master. Johnson, who tried in vain to prevent this marriage, thought that if not her virtue, at least her vice would have restrained her from it. The gloomy outcome of the long friendship between Johnson and Mrs. Thrale is further accented by a quotation which Boswell included from Mrs. Thrale's *Anecdotes* (published after Johnson's death) by saying that what made her "go on so long" with Johnson was pressure from her husband and what she admitted to be veneration of his talents and conversation; and she complained of the "terrifying" confinement during the last part of it. How different, commented Boswell, were these statements written after Johnson's death from what he had heard her say during his lifetime.

Boswell felt it his duty to set the record right and correct the erroneous impressions conveyed in Mrs. Thrale's book. He quoted

Malone as saying that Johnson was not given to speaking severely to people, as Mrs. Thrale reported; and he gave Malone's versions of the incidents that Mrs. Thrale mentioned. In answer to her charges that Johnson habitually refused help to persons whom he was too willing to advise, Boswell cited instances of his benevolence that were well known to the Thrales and their mutual friends. After dwelling at length on her errors, he apologized for having to "perform this unpleasant task." In light of his defense of Johnson against Mrs. Thrale's charges, it is impossible to understand why Boswell would write and publish a foolish poem supposedly written by Johnson, entitled *Ode by Dr. Samuel Johnson to Mrs. Thrale, Upon Their Supposed Approaching Nuptials*. It is more difficult to understand why he would include an excerpt of it in the *Life*, even if it was meant to illustrate an unsuccessful imitation of Johnson's style: "Shall, *catenated* by thy charms,/A captive in thy *ambient* arms,/*Perenially* be thine?"

Boswell presented Johnson in his last weeks as decaying in body but as mentally vigorous and alert. His intellectual stamina remained intact; his spirit, indomitable. Johnson participated energetically in the Fingal (Ossian) controversy by writing an answer to a pamphlet in support of its authenticity; he wrote Edward Dilly for books he wanted to read; he went to Oxford to visit his friend Dr. Adams, Master of Pembroke College, and the heads of two other colleges; and he made plans to translate into English the French historian Jacques-Auguste de Thou's *Historia Sui Temporis* and to write the life of Edmund Spenser.

It is to be regretted that, since Boswell left London for Scotland July 1, 1784, and did not return before Johnson's death December 13, information about him during this period must be found in letters from Johnson to Boswell and to Johnson's friends (when he was able to write) and to oral reports which Boswell later assembled. Some of the letters were written while Johnson was on a three-month jaunt to neighboring towns for the purpose of recovering his health. In a letter to his physician Dr. Brocklesby he stated that his dropsy had gone and that his asthma was "much remitted." His letters at this time, says Boswell, usually exhibited "a genuine and noble specimen of vigour and vavacity of mind, which neither age nor sickness could impair or diminish."

Johnson's fear of the unknown was familiar to all who knew him. Sir John Hawkins had insinuated in a "strange dark manner,"

Boswell charged, that this fear was due to "something of more than ordinary criminality weighing upon his conscience." Boswell thus set out to discharge "the most difficult and dangerous part of my biographical work" in defending Johnson's good name and at the same time fulfilling his obligation to truth and to "the interests of virtue and religion." He recalled that Johnson had had a similar concern when he represented Addison and Parnell as intemperate wine drinkers, but Boswell's speculations on Johnson's lapses from morality were nevertheless surprisingly straightforward.

He thought it no more than fair to mention Johnson's not-so-virtuous conduct when he first came to London and hobnobbed with Savage, going so far as accompanying prostitutes to taverns to hear their stories and almost certainly succumbing to temptations common to many a good and pious man. Pouring milk into tea on Good Friday, which plagued his conscience, was not the greatest of Johnson's sins; but, in violating what he professed to believe, he was no hypocrite. Boswell quoted from some of Johnson's prayers to show his distress of mind brought on by his sins—in short, his sincerity; and he insisted that Johnson could not be charged with dishonesty, malignancy, or badness of heart.

That Johnson's faith calmed him when near death was attested to not only by Dr. Brocklesby but by several others, including his servant Francis Barber. When he knew that he was not to recover except by a miracle, he refused further physic or opiates; for he wanted to render up his soul to God "unclouded." When he was handed a letter, he calmly mused that he would not be getting letters in the grave. A few days before the end he drew up his will, in which—after discharging his debts and making a few individual gifts and bequests—he left most of his money and personal effects to Barber. Ironically, Boswell had to report that Hawkins was the one to urge Johnson to make his will and to suggest Westminster Abbey as his place of burial. On the evening of December 13 the daughter of a friend came for his blessing. When she was ushered in, he turned around in the bed and uttered his last words: "God bless you, my dear!" Barber and Mrs. Desmoulins, sole survivors of his curious household, got up from their seats and, not hearing him breathe, realized that he was dead.

Boswell, had he been in London, no doubt would have given a more impressive account of the funeral than he does. Johnson's school fellow Dr. Taylor "performed the mournful office of reading the burial service." Of the persons present he could only report "a respectable number of his friends, particularly such members of the Literary Club as were then in town," and several of the Abbey's clergy. Burke, Windham, and Langton were among the pallbearers. Boswell was impressed with the Abbey as a "noble and renowned edifice," but his deep pride in his feudal connections moved him to assert that a poet or any man of imagination would wish to be buried there only if he had no "family sepulchure in which he can be laid with his fathers."

What this report of the funeral lacked in pomp and circumstance appropriate for the final tribute to a man of Johnson's stature was made up for in part by inclusion of other facts relating to Johnson's passing. Johnson, Boswell stated, had "abundant homage paid to him during his life," and "no writer in this nation ever had such an accumulation of literary honours after his death": many volumes of lives, memoirs, essays, poems. Furthermore, Oxford University honored him with a sermon in St. Mary's; and monuments were erected to him in St. Paul's Cathedral and in the cathedral in Lichfield, Johnson's birthplace.

Thinking that it would be expected of him, Boswell closed his monumental biography with a "character" of Johnson after the manner of eighteenth-century essayists and novelists; that is, he collected "into one view the capital and distinguishing features of this extraordinary man." Some of the sketch, he reminded his readers, he had already given in *The Journal of a Tour to the Hebrides*, and he had already presented in his biography illustrations of Johnson's characteristics which he was now summarizing: his large, clumsy physical appearance; his strange and uncouth mannerisms; his gloomy temperament; his vigorous mind and argumentative powers; his religious and moral earnestness; and his high-church and royalists sympathies. Boswell was at a loss in trying to recollect just how the death of Johnson, his "guide, philosopher, and Friend," did affect him; and he was compelled to resort to the expressed sentiments of "an eminent friend" who said of Johnson that his death had made a chasm which could not be filled and that we would have to "go to the next best"—for "no man can be said to put you in mind of Johnson."

CHAPTER 7

Peculiar Plan:
A Further View of the Life

BOSWELL intended to make his biography of Johnson as much of a life as possible—not complete in the sense of exhaustive, but as full and as true a re-creation of the man as could be achieved. He announced no particular period for special emphasis; yet four-fifths of the work deals with the last twenty years of Johnson's seventy-five years—the time when Boswell knew him—and half of it treats the last eight years.[1] This means that only one-half of the biography is devoted to the fifty-five years that encompass Johnson's childhood in Lichfield, his stay in Oxford University, the time he spent teaching school near Lichfield, and his struggling first years in London when he knew Savage. During this half century, he established himself as the distinguished author of *London, The Vanity of Human Wishes, The Rambler, The Idler, Irene*, the *Dictionary*, and *Rasselas*.

Boswell assiduously collected materials for Johnson's early life; but Sir John Hawkins, who was acquainted with Johnson during those early uncomfortable London years, treated this period more fully. He was with Johnson almost constantly just before his death, and he was therefore able to give also a better account of his last days.[2] It has been estimated that Boswell was in Johnson's company no more than 425 days, including the 101 days that they spent together on the trip to Scotland. In all, they were in the same neighborhood hardly more than two years.[3] Some of Johnson's letters to Boswell supplied information about his literary and other activities, but sometimes there were no letters for several months; indeed the lapse in correspondence once lasted well over a year. What is more, Johnson's letters frequently concerned Boswell more than they did himself. Eleven pages in the Hill-Powell edition of the *Life*, for instance, deal exclusively with the exchange of letters between them on the threats of Boswell's father to disinherit him.

Added to these limitations in biographical coverage is a disproportionate amount of space that Boswell gave to attacks on Hawkins's biography and on Mrs. Thrale's *Anecdotes of the Late Samuel
Johnson*. So sharp and sustained are his strictures against Hawkins
in the introduction that the controversial aspect of the work
might appear to assume an undue importance, and it is given
additional prominence by Boswell's frequently returning to the
attack throughout his book. For example, Boswell called attention
to Hawkins's charge that Johnson dissembled love for his wife;
to his failure to understand the real nature of Johnson's grief on the
death of his mother; to his erroneous statements about Garrick's
election to the Literary Club; to his inaccuracies concerning the
makeup of Johnson's Essex Head Club; to his aspersions against
Johnson's morals; and to other alleged inaccuracies and misrepresentations. The attacks on Mrs. Thrale's *Anecdotes* are primarily
concentrated in about ten pages, in which Boswell defends Johnson
against that lady's charges that he had rude manners and that he
would not bestir himself to give assistance to those who needed it.
Other attacks on Mrs. Thrale are also scattered throughout the
work.

This controversial phase of Boswell's *Life of Samuel Johnson*, the
disproportionate amount of space devoted to a short period, and the
occasional intrusion of the biographer's personal affairs into the
work—all of these add up to a biography strikingly unbalanced in
structure and uneven in pace. Yet Boswell remains to this day the
first of biographers, as Thomas Macaulay, who all but crowned him
the Prince of Dunces, was forced to admit.[4] Whatever, is the nature
of Boswell's achievement, he clearly understood it; for it was deliberate and not the accidental performance of a dunce. The uniqueness of his performance lies mainly in what he termed his "peculiar
plan of biographical representation." His distinctive employment
of conversation is the principal coefficient of that plan.

I   *The Place of Conversation in the* Life

As a record of truth or as a work of art, the *Life* must be judged
according to the writer's intentions and to the degree to which he
realized them; otherwise, its integrity will be overlooked. While
Boswell did seek strenuously to fill in the lacunae in the life story
of his subject for the years preceding their acquaintance, his primary
interest was a faithful recording of Johnson's conversation that he

himself had heard. "The principal store of wit and wisdom which this Work contains," he candidly stated, "was not a particular selection from his general conversation, but was merely his occasional talk at such times as I had the good fortune to be in his company."[5] This record was Boswell's chief aim, even if he did go out of his way to collect Johnson's other talk from anyone who had taken it down.

Boswell's "peculiar plan" was essentially an autobiographical approach to life-writing, for he used the term to refer to his own participation in Johnson's story. He made no mention of it when he discussed his biographical method in his introductory remarks, but he pointedly referred to it just before bringing the work to a close. In suffusing his distinctive treatment of conversation with this plan, he brought together two markedly original biographic techniques that make the *Life* a superlative achievement, one unique and ageneric, and thus the despair of anyone who would imitate him.

Boswell's skill was enhanced through his extensive knowledge of biographical literature. He was thus able carefully to think about what seemed to be the best way of constituting a good biography. His acquaintance also with works that owed their chief merit to conversation is added evidence of the artist enlightened in the literature of his craft. He praised the talk recorded in books by Plutach, Zenophon, and Valerius Maximus; the *Ana* which the French appended to accounts of celebrated persons; Selden's *Table Talk;* Drummond's conversations with Ben Jonson; and Spence's Anecdotes. Indeed, Boswell even wished that Shakespeare, Dryden, and other men of distinguished wisdom and wit had been attended by friends with sufficient taste to relish and with abilities enough to register, their conversation.[6]

When Boswell's critics viewed as a menace his diligence in taking down conversation, he answered them with a self-assurance induced by the knowledge that he had not cast his pearls before swine but had judiciously selected his subjects: "Few, very few, need be afraid that their sayings will be recorded. Can it be imagined that I would take the trouble to gather what grows on every hedge?"[7] When Sir William Scott invited Boswell to dinner, he enjoined his guest not to record their conversation lest he offend his other guests. Boswell thereupon decided to stay away, and, upon twice being asked to reconsider, he replied, seemingly without rancor, that he thought Scott and his friends should impress upon "persons of timidity and reserve" that his recording of the conversation of a man like Johnson "was a peculiar undertaking, attended with much anxiety and labour and that the conversations of people in general are by no means of that nature as to bear being registered."[8] And he wrote in the advertisement to the first edition: "The stretch of mind and prompt assiduity by which so many conversations were preserved, I myself, at some distance of time, contemplate with wonder."[9]

Boswell so did, however, revise some of the conversations as originally recorded in his Journal to give them a distinctive Johnsonian flavor.[10] At the same time, he preserved their original substance, language, and coloring. That his was a conscious artistry and not luck is hardly any longer a debatable point. This same artistry he applied to conversations of Johnson received second hand, especially when he had been away from London for longer periods than usual; and in the process he lost nothing of accuracy. Instead, he was able in this way to give, on the whole, a truer representation of Johnson—and a fuller one in the sense of rounding out his complete personality.

Boswell represents Johnson as never tiring to his listeners because of his extraordinary factual resourcefulness, his trenchant wit, and his dictatorial manner that was perhaps sometimes frightening but hardly ever dull. His conversational prowess in literature, philosophy, ethics, politics, and religion was well known; but it was pleasantly surprising to hear him hold forth also on practical arts like tanning, butchery, coining, brewing, and threshing. His wit was rugged and biting, especially as he directed it against the Scotch. When someone in his presence lamented the passing of "Old England," he retorted, "Sir, it is not so much to be lamented that Old England is lost as that the Scotch have found it." When a Scotsman one day at the Mitre made the mistake of praising Scotland's "many noble wild prospects," Johnson rebuffed him with, "But, Sir, let me tell you, the noblest prospect which a Scotchman ever sees, is the high road that leads him to England!" On being asked if he thought any man of a modern age could have written poems like *Ossian,* he replied, "Yes, Sir, many men, many women, and many children." He conceived of conversation as a contest, and his "forcible spirit and impetuosity of manner spared neither sex nor age." Although Boswell once saw him stun even Mrs. Thrale, he considered this rough trait in Johnson not altogether unattractive. On the contrary, it produced noble effects, investing him with the majestic appearance of "a lofty oak."

II   *Boswell No Mere Intruder*

The Life of Samuel Johnson is at times so crowded with Boswell's personal affairs and concerns that we might well wish him out of the way. More than eleven continuous pages in the Hill-Powell edition, for instance, are consumed with letters between Boswell and Johnson relating to Lord Auchinleck's intentions to disinherit him. Though exceptions to the rule, such brazen intrusions, sometimes utilized to fill in the gaps during Boswell's absence from London and from Johnson's company, are nevertheless objectionable; but we must not allow them to becloud our vision of the essential peculiarity of Boswell's place in the *Life,* which serves the better to illumine Johnson's character and personality and thus to give what Boswell said was more of a life than had ever been written.[11]

On Wednesday, July 20, 1763, two months after his first meeting with Johnson, Boswell entertained his uncle Dr. Boswell, Johnson, and Dempster at supper. Boswell reported nothing of Johnson's activities from July 21 until August 6, when Boswell left London, except the meetings and conversations that took place between the two of them alone. In the morning of July 21 he found Johnson in his quarters, and he drew him out on Hume's opposition to belief in miracles. At night they ate supper together at the Turk's Head coffee house, and Johnson spoke on his reading habits and his fondness for the acquaintance of young people, ways of relieving melancholy, Joseph Wharton's essay on Pope, maintaining subordination of rank, and other topics. Five days later they returned to the Turk's Head and dined in private, and Johnson talked about a number of things, but longest on the poet Samuel Derrick, a subject that Boswell introduced into the conversation. Johnson promised that on the following Saturday he would give Boswell suggestions for his course of studies while in Utrecht on his grand tour of the Continent. Boswell ended his account of this day by telling how, while he and Johnson walked "arm in arm" along the Strand, they were accosted by a prostitute. Johnson refrained from speaking harshly to her; and, as they strolled on, he talked of the misery sometimes caused by illicit relationships between the sexes.

After two days had passed, Boswell accompanied Johnson on a proposed excursion to Greenwich, where it was agreed that Johnson would give him the promised advice about his Utretch studies. A boy rowed the boat in which they sailed down the Thames, and they discoursed on Greek and Latin as requisites for a sound education. "What would you give to know about the Argonauts?" Johnson asked the boy; and, when he replied, "I would give what I have," Johnson was delighted with his answer; it illustrated, he thought, man's natural desire for knowledge. Boswell regretted his failure to record carefully Johnson's advice to him about his studies, the main business of the day. He could only recollect "with admiration an animating blaze of eloquence, which rouzed every intellectual power in me to the highest pitch, but must have dazzled me so much, that my memory could not preserve the substance of his discourse."

They spent a part of the evening walking in Greenwich Park; but, having no exquisite relish of the beauties of Nature and being more delighted with "the busy hum of men," they longed for Fleet Street. After sailing up the river on their return to London that night, when the air was cold and Boswell shivered while Johnson with his "robust frame" took it calmly, they concluded the day's excursion at the Turk's Head, talking about Auchinleck, the hereditary estate of the Boswell family. Just before seeing Johnson next day, Boswell had listened to a woman preaching at a meeting of Quakers. Telling his friend of his experience prompted the observation that "A woman's preaching is like a dog's walking on his hinder legs. It is not done well; but you are surprised to find it done at all." Some of Johnson's best sayings originated when he and Boswell conversed alone.

After a lapse of two days we find Johnson in Boswell's quarters, and later in the day Boswell joined him at tea with Mrs. Williams, who conversed well on a variety of literature. Johnson, who then took him on one of his favorite walks in the neighborhood, advised him to study Greek while abroad and to "read diligently the great book of mankind." The next day they sat together in the Turk's Head coffee house for the last time before Boswell left for the Continent. Johnson had told him several days before that he would accompany him to Harwich, for which port they accordingly departed early in the morning of the day before sailing time.

They traveled by stagecoach and had among their fellow passengers two talkative persons—a young Dutchman and a fat elderly lady, who spoke violently against the Inquisition, to the astonishment of all the passengers except Boswell. Johnson, who would sometimes yield to the devilish impulse of talking on either side of a question, defended the Inquisition by saying that false doctrine must be met head-on and that the state should join the church in punishing those who opposed the established religion. When the Dutchman lamented his country's custom of torturing accused persons in order to force them to confess, Johnson again took the unexpected position; he argued that torture in Holland was actually a favor to an accused man, for the evidence against him was no greater than what would amount to conviction in England; therefore, a Dutchman had at least one more chance than an Englishman to escape punishment.

While at supper that night Johnson expressed himself vehemently on the subject of eating, saying that "he who does not mind his own belly will not mind anything else." What did it matter that he had formerly spoken contemptuously of those who too anxiously minded their stomachs, or that he had even written one of his *Rambler* papers to say as much? Boswell used this occasion to describe for posterity one of Johnson's most unattractive habits: "When at table, he was totally absorbed in the business of the moment; his looks seemed riveted to his plate; nor would he, unless when in very high company, say one word, or even pay the least attention to what was said by others, till he had satisfied his appetite, which was so fierce and indulged with such intenseness, that while in the act of eating, the veins of his forehead swelled, and generally a strong perspiration was visible." To persons of delicate sensibilities, observed Boswell, such conduct could hardly fail to be disgusting, and it was hardly "suitable to the character of a philosopher." Johnson was, or liked to think he was, learned in the science of cookery; and Boswell took this opportunity to recount several anecdotes illustrating his interest in it.

Boswell and Johnson having arrived in Harwich, the place of Boswell's European departure, Boswell got his baggage aboard the packet boat to Holland and secured his passage. They went into the church, where Johnson sent Boswell to his knees before the altar to ask God's protection while away from his native country. Upon leaving the church, they talked of Bishop Berkeley's argument for the nonexistence of matter. Boswell was sure the theory was not true, yet he doubted the possibility of refuting it. "I shall never forget the alacrity with which Johnson answered, striking his foot with mighty force against a large stone, till be rebounded from it, 'I refute it *thus.*' "

Then they went down to the beach, where they parted affectionately. As the vessel put out to sea, Boswell kept his eyes upon
Johnson for a long time as Johnson "remained rolling his majestick
frame in his usual manner." Boswell saw him disappear as he walked
back into the town. Thus ends one of the most sustained, but not
untypical, narratives in the *Life* that treat exclusively of Boswell
and his subject Johnson. Boswell was not the intruder; the focus
was clearly on Johnson, who comes more fully alive in these
and similar accounts than in other portions of the work. The
result is ample justification of his "peculiar plan of biographical
representation."

Boswell's participation in (and sometimes manipulation of) Johnson's story was not confined to situations and events in which the
two alone functioned; it also encompassed occasions when others
were involved. Of this type of event in the *Life*, of which there
were many, the meeting of Johnson and Wilkes was the most out-
standing. Whatever the occasion, whoever the company, Boswell
was likely to function as a principal initiator of talk or as the provider
of points of departure from which Johnson would hold forth: "I thus
ventured to mention all the common objections against the Roman
Catholic Church, that I might hear so great a man upon them";
"I introduced the subject of death"; "I mentioned the petition to
Parliament for removing the subscription to the Thirty-Nine
Articles." In this way, Boswell started conversations on travel,
primitivism, subordination, necessity and freedom, immortality,
concubinage, dueling, and a host of other subjects. But Boswell's
most significant part in the *Life*, accounting for a sizable portion
of Johnson's best talk, remains the role that he played when alone
with Johnson.

It was not solely the richness of information or the usual interplay
of wit and personality to be enjoyed that prompted Boswell to
sound Johnson's depths; he was sometimes actuated by an urgent
wish for answers to his own psychological needs and queries. He
chose Johnson for biographical treatment in the first place because
of the ideas and the attitudes which he admired in him: notably, a
lively and continuous curiosity about all aspects of the human condition and a high regard for the good life. Since the light often
failed Boswell as he falteringly pursued the second ideal, his contemplation of Johnson's experience was for him a welcome deliverance. But, despite Boswell's own needs, the focus remained on

Johnson in the *Life.* For example, after they went to St. Clement's Church one Good Friday, as was their custom when Boswell was in London during Holy Week, they returned to Johnson's lodgings and drank tea with Mrs. Williams. Johnson then asked Boswell to go up with him to his study, "where we sat a long time together in a serene undisturbed frame of mind, sometimes in silence, and sometimes conversing, as we felt ourselves inclined, or more properly speaking, as *he* was inclined; for during all the course of my long intimacy with him, my respectful attention never abated, and my wish to hear him was such, that I constantly watched every dawning of communication from that great and illumined mind." It is Johnson, not Boswell, who dominates this scene. No less revealing of Johnson, since Boswell sought to present the whole man, was his rudeness to Boswell one day at Sir Joshua Reynolds's, where the presence of a number of people "by no means of the Johnsonian school" caused less attention to be paid him as was usual and consequently put him out of humor.

Despite Johnson's love of conversation as an exciting battle of wits, he liked talking with Boswell alone; and he anticipated his settling in London so they could have their talk at least once a week, for "That is the happiest conversation where there is no competition, no vanity, but a calm, quiet interchange of sentiments." When Boswell took leave of Johnson for what both feared might be their last farewell (since Johnson's health was declining fast), Johnson said to him in parting: "Were I in distress, there is no man to whom I should sooner come than to you. I should like to come and have a cottage in your park, toddle about, live mostly on milk, and be taken care of by Mrs. Boswell."

What turned out to be their actual final leave-taking is among the most vividly presented scenes in the biography. Boswell accompanied Johnson to his court entrance, and Johnson asked him if he would like to go with him into the house. He declined for fear that he would feel too depressed. After they affectionately told each other good-by in the carriage, Johnson got down to the pavement and called out "Fare you well." Without looking back, he "sprung away with a kind of pathetick briskness . . . which seemed to indicate a struggle to conceal uneasiness, and impress me with a foreboding of our long, long separation." Johnson died five and a half months later.

This very closeness of sympathy and understanding between

Boswell and Johnson, as well as Boswell's deftness in handling his material, helped to give unity to the work and thus to conceal or at least diminish the force of its organizational defects. The transition between the portion dealing with Johnson's life before the time of their first meeting and the latter part, for instance, is managed to avoid a noticeable change in tone and point of view. Since the actual writing of the biography was done many years after 1763, the year of the portentous meeting of the two, Boswell was able to infuse the Johnsonian "aether" with which it took him some time to become "impregnated."

The Boswell-Johnson relationship, moreover, is well represented in the pages preceding the account of their first meeting. In describing Samuel Johnson the boy, for instance, Boswell did not merely report what Johnson's step-daughter remarked concerning his exceptional memory as a child; he stated that he was in Johnson's presence when she said it. We are not just informed that Johnson received ten guineas for his poem *London*; we know that Johnson told Boswell about it and said that he would not have taken less. Boswell was only four years old when Johnson's *Life of Savage* came from the press, but he told of Reynolds's reaction to the book as if he had witnessed it himself. He did so by selecting only the telling details from Reynolds's account of the incident: he was so absorbed in the book as he leaned against the chimney piece that he was unable to lay it down until he had finished it; and, when he "attempted to move, he found his arm totally benumbed." A similar on-the-scene effect is managed in Boswell's story of the first and quite amusing encounter between Johnson and the painter and engraver Hogarth, when Hogarth saw him in Samuel Richardson's window shaking his head and rolling his body about in a ridiculous manner and thought he was an idiot committed to Richardson's watchful care.

The closeness of the Boswell-Johnson relationship precluded an objectivity quite as severe as that which Boswell announced at the outset of the biography. He said he would present facts and incidents wherever they fell chronologically and not attempt to group them for interpretive purposes. He accordingly refrained from bringing together correspondence between Johnson and his Negro servant Francis Barber, for instance, even though in so doing he would have afforded a more unified view of that correspondence. He stated that he would, instead, insert the letters "according to their dates." He withheld possible reasons for Johnson's trip to Oxford and Ashbourne, since Johnson had not given any reasons, because he wanted to avoid "the conjectural yet positive manner of writers, who are proud to account for every event which they relate."

Boswell, nevertheless, did sometimes group; and he did often evaluate and interpret, however unobtrusively he did so. In relating the founding of the Literary Club, he gave its history up to the time the *Life* was going to press in 1791; he marshaled eight pages of evidence to rescue Johnson from Mrs. Thrale's censures; and he used whatever evidence was available in making conjectures about irregularities in Johnson's conduct. Time and again he interpreted scenes by commenting on their significance. "The incident is here preserved," he wrote of a moment of hilarious laughter on Johnson's part, "that my readers may be acquainted even with the slightest occasional characteristics of so eminent a man." In this way, Boswell utilized the facts of Johnson's life to interpret him at his best or at his worst.

III   *The* Life *as Literary History: Another Phase of the Peculiar Plan*

Boswell's participation in Johnson's life story assumes additional significance because of his lifelong passion for the society of writers and wits and because of his own claims to membership in the select company of authors. He thus had excellent opportunities to enhance his work with what he termed on the title page of the third edition "A View of Literature and Literary Men in Great-Britain for Near Half a Century" during which Johnson flourished.[12] Boswell's membership in the Literary Club and his rather wide acquaintance with printers and booksellers further equipped him for his task, particularly since the work deals with literary men as well as with literature. In the spacious and well-appointed home of Charles and Edward Dilly, printers of his chief works, he enjoyed assemblies of wits more splendid than any other he attended save those at Sir Joshua Reynolds's and Henry Thrale's. He was on intimate terms with Alexander Donaldson, the Edinburgh publisher of his early works,[13] who later moved to London. Also there was William Strahan, the bookseller and close friend of of Johnson. It was through Thomas Davies, another bookseller, that the meeting of Boswell and Johnson was brought about.

The *Life of Samuel Johnson* is no life and times, for it affords only sporadic treatments of background events. Here is the pulse beat and the spirit of the times; but Boswell presents no in-depth discussions of movements and events. Johnson's very vivid description of the Gordon Riots, which were occasioned by Parliament's relaxation of the laws against Roman Catholics, is a notable exception.[14] Boswell's biography of Johnson is, rather, a great stage over which pass many of the distinguished literary personalities of Johnson's time, either as personages or as subjects of conversations. There are, as a matter of fact, valuable bits of literary history and criticism over and beyond what is promised on the title page. Literature and literary men that flourished before Johnson's time are treated in comments and anecdotes throughout the work. Certain names—classical, British, and continental—occur more frequently, in fact, than those of some of Johnson's contemporaries: Chaucer, Spenser, Shakespeare, Bacon, Milton, Dryden, and Addison, for instance; also Homer, Aeschylus, Horace, and Virgil; and Voltaire and Rousseau.

Among the members of the Literary Club, nearly all literary men, Goldsmith received the greatest attention in the *Life*[15]; but others in the group who also provided ballast for the literary-history phase of the work were Malone, Burke, Adam Smith, Reynolds, Steevens (The Shakespearean editor), Gibbon, and Percy (the antiquarian). Some of the best anecdotes and comments are, however, about persons not connected with Johnson's circle: James Thomson, an early contemporary of Johnson, and Lord Chesterfield, who flourished until eleven years before Johnson's death, come in for considerable attention. Pope, Gray, Swift, Richardson, and Fielding are not seen in Johnson's company, but they are alive in the talk of Johnson's group. Although William Cowper wrote good poetry before Johnson's death, his *Task* came afterward, as did the best poems of Robert Burns, and neither of these poets received any attention in the *Life*. William Blake was but twenty-seven years old at the time of Johnson's death, and his *Songs of Innocence* was not to appear for five years. Horace Walpole, who was very much alive and flourishing during Johnson's lifetime, curiously maintained an aloofness to Johnson and all but ignored his existence; mention of him in the biography is, therefore, but slight.

Johnson greatly admired Addison's prose and Pope's poetry, but he had a low opinion of Gray's poetry. He was not impressed with Addison's learning, but he believed that "his morality, his humour, and his elegant writing set him very high." He thought that Pope was as much admired as he had ever been; but, due to the great proliferation of books, which drew attention away from him, he was less read. On being told that Voltaire spoke of Pope as driving "a handsome chariot, with a couple of neat, trim nags; Dryden a coach and six stately horses," Johnson added that both drove coaches-and-six; but "Dryden's horses are either galloping or stumbling; Pope's go at a steady even trot." He thought, nevertheless, that there were passages in Dryden's poetry that derived "from a profundity that Pope could never reach."

We have seen how Boswell's enthusiasm for the society of wits and men of letters, his membership in Johnson's inner circle, and his acquaintance with printers and booksellers helped to qualify him for writing *The Life of Samuel Johnson* according to what he termed his "peculiar plan of biographical representation." In short, his literary interests and associations served him well in the writing of a work encompassing much literary history and comment. By considering his qualifications, we come closer to an understanding of the nature of his unsurpassed achievement in biographic art. But additional appreciation of his performance can be derived from an estimate of his intellectual equipment. He brought to bear upon his reading of literature a critical judgment by no means distinguished but one independent and solid enough to give interest and validity to his account of some of the most engaging wits and writers of history. And he expressed his views in prose that is so clear, unencumbered, and appropriate to the occasion that, within its context, it can hardly be estimated as other than distinguished. His critical comments on Johnson's works about English poets and other subjects and on those of some eighteenth-century and earlier writers are almost invariably judicious and are occasionally penetrating.

What intellectual equipment qualified him for such an impressive role? When as a very young man he published anonymously his *Ode to Tragedy* and dedicated it to "James Boswell," a man of "extensive erudition," he was having fun, not laboring under the illusion that he was learned or that anyone would think so. If from time to time, especially in his youth, he showed an inordinate fondness for the paraphernalia of learning, it was not so much to pretend to erudition as to enjoy the momentary fancy that he was learned. Real knowledge and genuine intellectual achievement he valued highly, never confusing the appearance for the actuality and never satisfied with tinkling brass as a substitute for solid gold. The oft-recurring frank admissions in his Journal, letters, and published works about his intellectual limitations attest to a lifelong unwavering standard of excellence and to an abiding dissatisfaction with his failure to measure up to his own high standards. What he aspired to be but was not brought him little comfort; and, as if he feared that his occasional "egotism and self-applause" would be taken seriously—how ridiculous he managed to make himself at times!—he disarmed his critics by announcing that such actions were performed "with a conscious smile."[16]

Having missed solid learning, Boswell had to settle, whether satisfied or not, for the next best thing: a fairly good acquaintance with the tried and proved ancient and modern authors (especially British) in the original, in translation, or in both. And he knew enough Latin to engage every now and then in learned talk, even if it was sometimes wistful. Coming perhaps closer to the truth than his self-depreciating nostalgia for the learning he never acquired was his candid assertion at the end of his *Hypochondriack* series, as he looked back on what he had written, that it was more learned than he had expected it would be.[17] More just, in fact, was the estimate of himself that he gave in *The Journal of a Tour to the Hebrides*: that he "had thought more than anybody supposed, and had a pretty good stock of general learning and knowledge." On his return to England from his grand tour, Johnson complimented him, as we have noted, on his "general knowledge of Books and men."

Boswell deserves no credit, however, for having been born in an age that provided an excellent background for his peculiar achievement. His was the century when biographical writing came into its own, when many distinguished full-length biographies, as well as collections of short lives, were written. We may cite, for instance, George Cavendish's *Cardinal Wolsey*, William Roper's *Sir Thomas More*, Dryden's and Walton's *Lives*, George Nicol's *Biographia Britannia*, and Johnson's *Life of Savage* and *Lives of the Poets*. Boswell said in the opening sentence of his *Life of Samuel Johnson* that Johnson himself excelled all other men in the writing of the lives of others. It was for Boswell to enrich himself with this ample harvest and to elevate biographic art from commemorative and panegyric to full and true representations of a life. Given as he was to indulging in wild fancy, he was to profit from his century's respect for restraint, reason, and demonstrable truth—virtues which he himself greatly admired and which, therefore, served as steadying influences. The neoclassical emphasis upon realism and actuality as opposed to vague romanticizing and imaginative flights also helped to shape his thinking and determine his biographical method. His veneration for the truth received abundant sanction from Johnson, to whose biography he brought his subject's imperfections as well as positive virtues.

Boswell not only had read enough and experienced enough by the time he began his associations with the wits of Johnson's circle; he also had interests sufficiently broad for him to have opinions of his own and to defend them with confidence. Several criticial encounters with Johnson, encounters that constitute some of the critical material of the biography, are cases in point; and they are interspersed throughout the work. We have, for example, the matter of James Macpherson's *Fragments of Ancient Poetry*, which when it first appeared impressed Boswell, who wrote to Andrew Erskine that it made him feel that he had a soul. He even went so far as to contribute to a fund to enable Macpherson to search in the Highlands and the Hebrides for "a long poem in the Erse language" reputed to be preserved somewhere in those regions. But, when the epic appeared in six books, each having "a perpetual recurrance of the same image" that had appeared in the fragments, and when Macpherson, upon request, had failed to bring forth a manuscript in authenticity or merit to the epic, Boswell hastened to comment in a footnote: "I desire not to be understood as agreeing *entirely* with the opinions of Dr. Johnson, which I relate without any remark. The many imitations of *Fingal*, that have been published, however, confirm this observation in a considerable degree."[18]

Johnson, not Boswell, has come down to us as one of England's great critics; yet Boswell, because he was more independent of the prescriptive criticism of his age than Johnson was, may impress twentieth-century readers as occasionally revealing a truer taste than that of his distinguished friend. His opposition to Johnson's strictures on ornamental architecture and sculpture ("statuary") is a case in point. To Dr. Johnson, the labor required by these two arts was disproportionate to their utility. Painting, he held, did not consume labor incommensurate with the results; "but a fellow will hack half a year at the block of marble to make something in Stone that resembles a man." This view, thought Boswell, was "a Gothic reflection, for certainly statuary is a noble Art of imitation and preserves the utmost expression of the human frame."

Boswell believed that the reason for Johnson's negative response to the poems of William Hamilton was that their beauties were "too delicate for the Doctor's robust perceptions," and he agreed with Garrick that Johnson lacked taste for "the finest productions of genius." Johnson's opinions that playacting was nothing more than repeating evoked a similar reaction. An actor only "clasps a hump on his back and a lump on his leg and cries, 'I am Richard the Third' "; the art of a ballad singer is higher, for he sings as well as repeats. Boswell labeled this statement "the most fallacious reasoning," holding that actors, representing "exalted characters" and touching "the noblest passions," possessed powers deserving of the highest respect.

As they discussed a number of British writers, Boswell never gave in to Johnson's opinion if he believed his judgment on the point in question was superior to Johnson's. For the attack he would, indeed, solicit the aid of like-minded persons present; but, owing to the reputation of their formidable opponent, their efforts were generally failures. Such was the case at the Literary Club one evening when Swift was the topic of conversation. For many years Boswell had numbered him among his favorite authors, but Johnson always, as on this occasion, attacked the Dean. He was expressing then the view that, excepting the Inventory of the Man Mountain in *Gulliver's Travels*, Swift's writings were usually so poor that it was difficult to believe he had written *A Tale of a Tub*. "I was keen for Swift," wrote Boswell, "and tried to rally the troops, but in vain. They durst not engage Mr. Johnson."

Perhaps Johnson's and Boswell's best-known critical argument was about Richardson and Fielding. Johnson held that the persons in Fielding's novels were mere characters of manners and, as such, could be understood by a superficial observer; but, in order to comprehend Richardson's characters of nature, one must "dive into the recesses of human nature." He was especially impressed with the quality of Richardson's psychology, holding that there was "more knowledge of the heart in one letter of Richardson's" than in all of Fielding's *Tom Jones*.

Boswell shared Johnson's respect for Richardson's knowledge of the heart, but he was amazed that he would so underrate *Tom Jones*, which, because of its sentiments, story, and variety of diction and execution throughout, had stood the test of public opinion. He saw in Fielding a superior picture of life and a benevolence of greater merit than all the sentimental protestations in Richardson's novels. The following statement of Boswell bespeaks a clear-headed reader—one not taken in by Pamela's false sentiment but impressed by the genuine character underneath Tom's coarse exterior:

Fielding's characters, though they do not expand themselves so widely in dissertation, are just pictures of human nature, and I will venture to say, have more striking features, and nicer touches of the pencil. . . . I will venture to add, that the moral tendency in Fielding's writings, though it does not encourage a strained and rarely possible virtue, is ever favourable to honour and honesty, and cherishes the benevolent and generous affections. He who is as good as Fielding would make him, is an amiable member of society and may be led on by more regulated manners, to a higher state of ethical perfection.[19]

It is not surprising to find Boswell appreciating the boisterous high spirits of the characters that peopled Fielding's world and praising his "humour and practical knowledge of life in its most active scenes and its most convivial gaiety."[20]

Another biography such as the *Life* may never again appear, for there may never again be such a concomitance of factors as went into the making of Boswell's biography: a subject splendidly suited to the biographer's interests and ideals, a style that fitted the word to the thought and act, a milieu that served both to modify the author's negative traits and nourish his virtues, and the genius that perceived the uniqueness of his task, the patience and industry to pursue it in the face of dismal personal defeat, and the boldness to fuse his own life and story into his subject's story.

IV *Unhappy Postlude*

When Boswell's great undertaking became a task fulfilled, he lost his élan. So used to expecting an elevation of spirit, he was merely going through the motions of looking upward. From the time his biography came off the press until his death four years later, he presented at least a fairly normal front to his friends. After all, he did receive recognition for his achievement; and his financial situation was improved. So encouraged was he, in fact, that upon publication of the second edition, he had printed, for the accommodation of the purchasers of the first edition, *The Principal Cor-*

*rections and Additions of the First Edition of Mr. Boswell's Life of
Johnson* (1783). But in spite of his success, his hold on life was
gradually weakening. He avoided meeting people in the streets lest
they notice how "insufficient and troubled" he was. When he went
down to Cornwall to visit his friend Temple and the two "rode
calmly between his churches, I observed that he held a creditable
actual station in Society, whereas I held none. Yet we both agreed
that I was better as a distinguished Biographer than as a Lord of
Session."

He would occasionally experience something of his old stimulation when he thought there might be an interesting literary project
in the offing. Being an active member of the Royal Academy Club,
he was accustomed to dining at their meeting place, where were to
be found men of "talents and celebrity." On December 21, 1792,
at one of the dinners, he sat next to Sir William Chambers, who,
with the approval of the members present, expressed the wish that
Boswell would write the history of the academy and provide biographical sketches for the deceased members. We also observe his
contemplating at this time whether to publish his travels after being
encouraged by Wilkes to undertake the project. Nothing, though,
seemed to bring back his old enthusiasm, his old lively expectations.
There were still good meetings at the Literary Club, for Burke and
some other able men were yet members. Nevertheless, lamented
Boswell, he had lost his faculty for recording conversation. In fact,
he had "little relish even for the Club. I enjoy chiefly the wine."

At this time, he sent only a few items to the newspapers and magazines. In a letter to the *Gentleman's Magazine*[21] he defended the
justice of Johnson's "animadiversion" upon the Reverend Mr.
and Mrs. Gastrell for cutting down Shakespeare's mulberry tree,
and we find him again coming to Johnson's defense against the
attack of Miss Ann Seward of Lichfield, who disapproved of
Johnson's strictures on some of Milton's poetry.[22] In another letter
to the *Gentleman's Magazine*,[23] he disagreed with Miss Seward
on the curious point as to whether or not Johnson was actually
supposed to have written at the tender age of three some verses on
a duck and certain others about a sprig of myrtle.

Until the very day before one of his last attacks compelled him
to leave a meeting of the Literary Club, he concerned himself with
matters pertaining to an appropriate epitaph for Johnson's monument in Westminister Abbey. The life of the man whom he had

done most to preserve for posterity he was still endeavoring to honor, even though, as far as the records seem to suggest, he no longer saw fit to record his own. He held that he should live no more than he was able to record of his life, "as one should not have more corn growing than one can get in." It is a curious fact, therefore, that, after the date of the last entry in his Journal—April 12, 1794—his letters and miscellaneous items suggest little that was worth recording.

He was unable to read a letter from Temple in the middle of May 1795. Three days later, May 19, he died. His body was taken back to Auchinleck for burial in the family vault, not long after his cousin had urged him to return to Auchinleck and he had replied that he would—"alive or dead."[24]

CHAPTER 8

Boswell's Life of Boswell

B OSWELL said that his biography of Johnson would be the fullest life of a man ever written, but he wrote one of himself that is even fuller. Upon the private printing of the eighteen volumes of his Journals and other documents,[1] he became, as J. W. Krutch stated it, "perhaps the best self-documented man in all history."[2] A massive accumulation of materials made this documentation possible. In 1926 an American collector, Lieutenant Colonel Ralph Isham, visited Malahide Castle in Ireland and returned with a bulky batch of freshly discovered private papers and journals, among which were manuscripts, letters, and notes covering the unbelievably wide area of activities that included accounts of Boswell's life as early as 1754, his journey to the Continent and to Corsica in 1763-65, his relations with the nobility in the courts and drawing rooms of England and Europe and with distinguished statesmen and men and women of letters, and his preparation of the *Life of Samuel Johnson*.

Additional papers were later found both at Malahide Castle in Ireland and at Fettercairn House, Kincardineshire, Scotland. Some of this material was acquired by Colonel Isham; and, together with the Malahide Papers, the collection became known as the Isham Collection, which later came into the possession of Yale University. The treasure of Boswellian materials, in fact, was already in the making a century ago when a large bundle of Boswell's letters to Temple was accidentally found in Boulogne, France.

These and other materials, which are being issued by Yale University in trade and research editions,[3] constitute the main body of Boswell's own life story; but some of the works that he himself published enlarge still further this mass of autobiographical data; for example, his *Journal of a Tour to Corsica*; essays in *The London Magazine* and other periodicals; and, notably, *The Journal of a Tour to the Hebrides* and *The Life of Samuel Johnson, LL.D.* His coauthorship of the published *Letters between The Honourable*

Andrew Erskine, and James Boswell, Esq., a juvenile performance, should not be entirely discounted. Four years before his death he published his *Memoirs* in the *European Magazine*[4] in two installments of about four pages each. This brief sketch and a long letter that he wrote to Rousseau while in his mid-twenties[5] must be added to this enormous accumulation of data, as well as countless other letters, not a few of which have been published since his death.[6]

I   *The Search for Self*

Boswell's Journals, which comprise the bulk of his autobiographical writings, must be viewed in terms of their relation to truth and of their literary value. He began keeping a Journal in 1758, but the first continuous one was not started until 1762. He kept it up until about thirteen months before his death, publishing only those parts covering the Corsica and Hebrides journeys and adapting other portions for inclusion in the *Life of Samuel Johnson*. The validity of the Journals as a contribution to a true life can hardly be assessed without taking into consideration Boswell's reasons for writing those that he did not publish and ascertaining whether he intended ever to publish either all or some of them.

Three years before the end of Boswell's life, Wilkes suggested that he publish his travels; and he pondered what to do.[7] That he did not rule out the possibility of publication after his death is evident in the provisions of his will concerning the materials preserved in the "cabinet" at Auchinleck: "I hereby leave to . . . Sir Williams Forbes, the Reverend Mr. Temple, and Edmond Malone, Esquire, all my manuscripts of my own composition, and all my letters from various persons, to be published for the benefit of my younger children, as they decide, that is, to say, they are to have discretionary power to publish more or less."[8] Boswell knew he was bequeathing to the world an exceptional record of a life and that his Journal should not, therefore, go to waste: "My journal will afford materials for a very curious narrative."[9]

Although his Journal was private and uninhibited (since he was passionately committed to the recording of the truth about himself), he wrote parts of it not only for his own but for others' eyes—but not necessarily for publication. In introductory remarks in his first sustained Journal, "The Journal of My Jaunt—Harvest 1762," he stated that it was written for William McQuae, a young, well-educated clergyman and close friend of his who had served as tutor in the Auchinleck household, and for John Johnston, the somewhat older laird of Grange, who for many years was Boswell's intimate associate and correspondent. At the beginning of his *London Journal* of 1762-63, he wrote that it was for John Johnston.

We cannot escape the conclusion that Boswell never intended to publish any portion of his Journal except two specially prepared accounts of travel (one to Corsica; the other to the Hebrides). The question remains, then, why did he, during virtually all of his adult life, so conscientiously apply himself to his Journal? Time and again he stated that he did so in order to discover what kind of person he was, or was becoming, by recording as completely as possible a register of his mental states, to improve himself and therefore grow into the sort of person he wanted to be, and to derive pleasure from it.

"Know thyself," he wrote, for "surely this knowledge is of all the most important"; and there is no better way for a man to know himself than by "attending to the feelings of his heart and to his external actions. . . . I have therefore determined to keep a daily journal in which I shall set down my various conduct which will be not only useful but very agreeable."[10] His Journal (like those of some Puritans of his day who kept journals as a means of soul-searching) would make him "do well" since he was to record his actions. The time and attention given to his Journal would itself have a salutary effect in keeping him from indolence and hypochondria, and it would help him store up enjoyment for the future: "Very often we have more pleasure in reflecting on agreeable scenes that we have been in than we had from the scenes themselves."

Of these three purposes, the foremost for Boswell seems to have been the recording of the states of his mind, already a favorite pastime when Johnson advised him to go about it diligently. In his efforts to form himself "into a man," he used his Journal as a psychograph. What he invariably saw was an amazing changeableness that disturbed him and, at the same time fascinated him with its promise of infinite possibilities. It was not alone the question of who he was that intrigued him but the contemplation of what he was becoming: "I have a singular kind of Philosophy," he wrote in his Journal, "which will make me content to be whatever I shall turn out."

Boswell's approach to the recording of his life was more that of a diarist (which he was essentially) than that of a person who sets out to present a narrative of his life. In other words, it was not a long-range approach[11]—not, at least, in the common acceptance of the term. He focused his attention on the interest of the moment; but he did not, like Rousseau and Augustine, follow a plan of revealing himself by means of the confession. Nor did he, like Wordsworth, attempt to trace the growth of his mind. His interest in the nature of his mind and in the discovery of his true self, nevertheless, lends a unity of purpose to a large portion of the record of himself that he left to the world. He raised more questions about himself than he was able to answer, but the efforts to find the answers were not all in vain.

At times, his pronouncements were flamboyant. Derived from a sure and steady search, they were, nevertheless, generally correct. Speaking of himself in the third person, he wrote that he "had travelled a good deal, and seen many varieties of human life. He had thought more than any body supposed, and had a pretty good stock of general learning and knowledge."[12] In these two statements, made in his third year, he succinctly named the activities and personal equipment that qualified him for one of the superlative accomplishments of his age.

Developments in the economic, political, religious, social, and literary life of England in the eighteenth century formed the backdrop for the century's ideas; and in these areas of activity the best minds in Britain were at work. Much was said and written on the evils or advantages of luxury, the benefits of country or city life, and the nobility or depravity of the savage. Slavery, which existed on a small scale in England itself, and the slave trade came in for a share of attention, as did also subordination in government and society, American independence, the French Revolution, predestination and free will, immortality, and other theological and ecclesiastical questions. These and many other topics recurred frequently in Boswell's private Journals and reappeared in his published works, especially in the *Life of Johnson*, from the onset of his career until its close.

"The Journal of My Jaunt—Harvest 1762"[13] is the earliest of Journals to which we have access, and it is not among those printed in the Yale editions. Covering the period between September 14 to November 14, 1762, it recounts Boswell's experiences and impressions while on a two-month ramble on horseback in and near his native Ayrshire. He was accompanied by his father's fellowjudge and good friend Lord Kames (Henry Home), and they visited many country estates of relatives and old friends. He described a number of picturesque estates—like Kenmore, for instance, where the house was on a beautiful hill behind which were wild mountains and woods and a river that ran into a seven-mile lake.

There is a fresh charm in Boswell's slightly self-conscious style as he reports his experiences in these delightful settings. As a fledgling journal writer, he was highly successful both in his selection of what to record and in his apt descriptions and rather mature observations of people. At one of the farm houses we see him taking part in an end-of-the-harvest merrymaking, dancing with all his might with the housekeeper and little chambermaid. We learn that tutors in most families were treated little better than livery servants and walked around as if they were condemned criminals. Boswell is already recording his rapidly shifting mental states; discussing Johnson's style; longing to keep his mind lively and gay with London's "infinite variety"; expressing veneration for old families, highland clans, and Scottish ancestors; deriving much pleasure from keeping a journal and recording conversation; and joining Erskine in the cultivating of a literary friendship with David Hume.

II *The Yale Trade Editions of the Boswell Papers*

The first of the Yale editions of the Private Papers of James Boswell is *Boswell's London Journal, 1762-63*, edited by Frederick A. Pottle (1956). It records Boswell's activities from the time he left Scotland on November 15 until August 4, his last day in London before setting out on his grand tour. A work of distinct literary merit, one in which Boswell paid greater attention to structure and style than in any other sustained piece of writing, it contains the account of his first meeting with Johnson, the long suspense story of his affair with an actress, and reports of a succession of interviews relating to his efforts to get a commission in the Guards and thus establish himself in London.

As Boswell left Edinburgh, he rode along in a small carriage with a chance acquaintance, the son of a Jacobite who had participated in the Rebellion of 1745; and he glowed with Scotch pride. But, four days later, he rejoiced when he beheld London in the distance, and he quoted Cato on the immortality of the soul. Immediately after arriving in the city, he plunged into the world of literary men and social gadabouts, first paying respects to Dr. John Pringle, Scots friend of Benjamin Franklin and distinguished physician; then he paid his respects to the rakish tenth earl of Eglinton, lord of the bedchamber and friend of the duke of York, the king's brother, at whose invitation he went to the House of Lords to hear the king open Parliament. He attended a gathering at Lord Eglinton's, where he saw the chancellor of the University of Oxford, the prince of Mecklenburg (the queen's brother), and a company of dukes and duchesses.

Later in the evening he was at a "rout" at the magnificent Northumberland House, where he was dazzled by the sight of three or four hundred persons of rank and fashion. Himself from an ancient Scottish family, he could boast of unquestioned social connections, which he fully exploited in his pursuit of a commision in the Guards, frequently importuning the duke of Queensberry and the countess of Northumberland to intercede in his behalf. He shunned the coarse raillery of his Scottish friends Erskine and Dempster, wishing instead to assume the dignified and restrained character of Addison and to be more often in the company of Lord Eglinton.

That Boswell thought of himself as the hero of a structured story is evident throughout this most literary portion of his long Journal. "Let me consider that the hero of a romance or novel must not go uniformly along in bliss, but the story must be chequered with bad fortune." Obviously fancying himself to be Captain Macheath in *The Beggar's Opera,* which he all but knew by heart, he disguised himself one night as a blackguard. He wore buckskin britches and carried an old oaken stick, went out and picked up a prostitute in the park, and accosted several others before the night was over, barely escaping arrest. Temple, whose companionship he often enjoyed during this London visit, was no doubt correct when he declared that Boswell's Journal made him hunt about for adventures to adorn it with. He compared himself with Aeneas, who met with many disasters while on his way to Italy. Why could Boswell not do the same as he pursued "the chase of happiness"?

The rise and fall of the action is particularly noticeable in Boswell's attempts to meet Samuel Johnson, to come to grips with himself relative to whether he would follow a career in Scotland or London, to throw off his Scots ways while eschewing the boisterous company of Scots acquaintances and friends in London and to achieve English manners, to become a man of ideas and letters, to consummate several assignations—most noticeably the one with Louisa—and to attain moral and intellectual stability and thus learn which one of the many possible Boswells he could become.

Boswell skillfully created suspense in his story of intrigue with a Covent Garden actress whom he called Louisa. When he visited her for the first time, he announced his wish to establish a friendship; and, as he took his leave, he felt uneasy but hopeful. He met with only faint encouragement on the next few visits, but his hopes were raised just enough to keep him hanging on. Each time he would set a day for his return, and on each visit the talk became increasingly intimate. As the day of bliss arrived, the excitement of it all induced in him the curious fear that he might prove impotent. The sound of Louisa's landlady coming up the stairs prevented this embarrassing and ironic outcome of events. After several more near successes, they arranged to meet at an inn. Boswell graphically described the occasion. The supper and wine and the merry bells of close-by St. Bride's Church formed a fit accompaniment to his exhibition of "godlike vigor," which, he was pleased to report, amazed Louisa. The relationship lasted several weeks, but it ended abruptly when Boswell discovered that he had become a victim of venereal contamination.

Day after day, week after week, we see Boswell frantically pressing for a commission in the Guards. When the duke of Queensberry and the duchess of Northumberland, to whom he directed most of his efforts, finally tired of him; he had to abandon the pursuit; and he refused to consider a military assignment that would have necessitated his living away from the English capital. Meanwhile, he got his father's consent to spend the winter in Utrecht, Holland, to study law and then visit elsewhere on the Continent. While yet in London he managed, after several attempts, to be introduced to Samuel Johnson,[14] and in the following weeks he filled many pages of his Journal with conversations of Johnson and the men of his circle, which he later utilized in his biography of Johnson. He chose Child's coffee house as a weekly retreat, mainly because it had been a favorite with Addison. Here on Saturdays he read *The North Briton* and then visited Dempster and Erskine and discussed the works that they planned to publish in collaboration.[15] This periodic ritual routine was his initiation into the world of letters, the best of his worlds.

In the next three Yale editions, Boswell gives accounts of his grand tour of Europe from 1763 to 1766. He went to Holland, Germany, Switzerland, Corsica, Italy, and France. Such a trip must have been especially exciting to a young man of his century, which was an age of exploitation and discovery, extensive commerical and colonial expansion, and increased travel and communication. Britain lost America but took over Canada and much of India and began settling in Australia. Acceleration of international traffic in ideas, customs, and goods was inevitable. Cultivated Englishmen, accustomed already to making the grand tour of the Continent, now extended their wanderlust to include other lands; and they further satisfied their growing curiosity by reading and discussing travel accounts and by talking with travelers.

Boswell's appetite for acquaintance with foreign men and manners led him to explore all the ways of satisfying it. Just as one movement of a symphony might capture its essential quality better than the others, Boswell's interest in travel and in what could be learned from it reflects better than any other of his characteristics his essential and distinctive personality. Here we can best see at play his curiosity, enthusiasm, and acute awareness—characteristics which inform much of his writing about himself and about Johnson and their friends and which constitute its enduring freshness.

Boswell in Holland, 1763-64, edited by Frederick A. Pottle (1952), presents accounts of Boswell's stay in Holland from August, 1763, to the following June. Since he lost all but a very small portion of his Holland Journal, these accounts have been reconstructed mainly from letters and frequent memoranda which he wrote to himself each morning. These memoranda contained brief reviews of each previous day's activities and advice to himself, written in the second person, for the present day. He started them before he left London, instructing himself to study in earnest while in Utrecht but "not to be as much a student as a traveller." He cautioned himself to be constantly "reserved and calm," to be prudent if not good, and to remember Johnson's precepts and to so conduct himself that he would be able to return to Auchinleck with dignity.

Hardly had Boswell reached Holland before he wrote John Johnston a long letter saying he had left exciting London "with a

heavy heart" and was on his way to a dull Dutch university town
only to comply with his father's wishes. Utrecht's gloominess
affected him so negatively that while on a brief trip to nearby
Rotterdam he groaned aloud in the street and doubted that he could
endure Utrecht. Reassured by advice from one of the *Rambler*
papers to beware of miseries attendant upon unemployed minds,
he resolved to study six hours a day and to "act with fortitude."
In a letter to Temple, we learn that he rose at seven, read Ovid
until nine, ate breakfast, and from ten to eleven read Tacitus. He
attended a lecture in civil law from noon to one o'clock, and from
three to four he sat with his French master. His victory over idleness
and dissipation spurred him on to greater efforts at stability. Thus
his "Inviolable Plan," in which he tells himself to accept the good
advice of Temple, Johnson, and his father and to settle on a fixed
way of avoiding these vices in order to prepare himself for a stable
career in Edinburgh as a lawyer and for maintaining his dignity as
the eventual laird of Auchinleck. Except for occasional visits to
Amsterdam for a girl, he maintained a strict regimen throughout
his stay in Holland. But he never allowed his studies to interfere
with his enjoyment of the social activities that turned Utrecht,
during its social season, into a gay city. After all, he wrote, foreign
manners were a part of his studies.

Excellent opportunities to study such manners were abundantly
available to him. On a visit to The Hague, he met the wealthy
Sommelsdicks, his father's relatives who had distinguished themselves in literature and politics; he called on the British ambassador;
and he supped twice with the prince of Strelitz, the English queen's
brother. In Utrecht his social life was first centered at the home of
the Reverend Robert Brown, Scots minister of the Presbyterian
church there. The circle later grew, particularly during the social
season, to include brilliant semiweekly card assemblies and almost
nightly parties. With a sustained journal missing, we are especially
indebted to three other media (in addition to letters, notes, and
memoranda) containing observations and valuable references to
his daily activities: frequent French and Dutch themes and ten
lines of poetry a day. For three weeks straight he once plied his
verses without missing a day.

In his ten lines for October 31, 1763, Boswell announced that a
certain Utrecht lady was making his "gay bosom beat with love's
alarms." And thus began the longest love affair of his life. The

lady referred to was Isabella Agneta Elizabeth van Tuyll van Serooskerken, known also as Belle de Zuylen, or, more familiarly, as Zelide, whose family had held a respected social position in Holland for six hundred years. Subsequent references to Zelide were not so frequent as might be expected, and it was some time before they increased in number or in warmth of affection. Her incessant chatter and freely expressed libertine views of love and marriage annoyed Boswell no end. Furthermore, their relationship was complicated by Boswell's strong feelings for the rich and attractive Catherine Geelvinck ("la Veuve"), friend of Zelide. The capricious course of his and Zelide's affair, which was marked more by quarrels than by evidence of genuine feeling, forms the chief line of action in this volume. By the time Boswell left Holland, this affair had hardly progressed beyond a contest in coyness, but gradually coyness gave way to serious doubts as to the compatibility of their ideas and temperaments.

June, 1764, marks the end of the time represented in this volume, but the editor includes the correspondence of or about Zelide and Boswell for as late as 1769, affording the reader a connected story of their courtship. Boswell's interest in her took a sharp turn upward when she wrote that there was a man whom she thought of constantly and loved "much," but he had never proposed to her. When Boswell wrote to her insisting that she frankly admit her passion for him, she replied that she was shocked by his "puerile vanity" and by his "arrogant rigidity." She would have understood this "amiable and proud Scot," he answered, if she had possessed greater knowledge of the human heart.

Even after Zelide informed Boswell that the gentleman had proposed, Boswell was, or pretended to be, fully determined to marry her; and he wrote her father saying he thought she would be a fitting wife to the heir of an ancient family. When Zelide visited London and made no attempt to get in touch with Boswell, who had returned to Scotland after his European travels, it appeared that there would be no more correspondence between them; but it was briefly renewed in 1768. She had found him "odd and loveable," and a number of times he wrote frantically of his passion for her, but in his Journal and letters he never appears to be deeply in love with Zelide. Their long affair appropriately ended in a whimper. Zelide, who eventually found seclusion in a marriage of arrangement and subsequently had several love affairs, 'joined the ranks of distinguished eighteenth-century letter writers through her correspondence with Constant d'Hermanches and Benjamin Constant; and she wrote *Caliste*, a successful novel.

The second Yale edition devoted to Boswell's travels is *Boswell on the Grand Tour: Germany and Switzerland, 1764*, edited by Frederick A. Pottle (1953). Boswell left Utrecht in June, 1764, traveling with George Keith, tenth earl of Marishal, with whom it was prearranged that he would tour Germany, and with a strangely silent Turkish woman whom Marishal had adopted when she was a girl. Marishal had a distinguished career, first as an officer under the duke of Marlborough, as a leader in the Jacobite rebellion, and as the Prussian Frederick the Great's ambassador to Paris and also Madrid. Boswell was proud to be traveling with so distinguished a Scot, of whom he took leave in the latter part of September and proceeded on to Switzerland, passing through many German cities on his way out of the country. Germany in the eighteenth century was made up of what was later Austria and is now the divided Germany and Czechoslovakia. It was presided over by an emperor elected by nine electors, each of whom in turn presided over a magnificent court comprising, however, only a small territory.

This book, made up mainly of Boswell's "Journal of a Tour Through the Courts of Germany," is easily his most exciting travel narrative. He lived in incommodious and drab inns, twice sleeping on straw; but he spent more time amid royal splendor, dining, playing whist, and dancing in palaces. He saw the king of Prussia walking majestically in the midst of submissively bending officers, and he madly tried for days to arrange to be presented to him, but he was unsuccessful. He attended a wedding in Berlin and saw the bride standing in the center while a ring of men danced around her, and he attended a party at the home of a member of the king's War Council, where his wife with "health most florid in her face" ran from table to table with bottles in her hand and was "quite the female Bacchanalian." At Coswig, Boswell was accused by one of the castle guards of being a political spy and was promptly taken into custody but was freed later by the burgemeister.

He spent much time with a number of other impressive Scots (in addition to Marishal): Andrew Mitchel, Frederick the Great's close friend and minister plenipotentiary; the hearty Captain Scott, who for a number of years had been in the service of the prince of Prussia; and the "honest, spirited" Highlander Lauchlan

Macpherson. These men made him proud of Scotland. Yet he wrote
to Temple that the thought of returning to Scotland filled him with
terror, for there he would become an advocate and "be excelled
by sober judges who have not half my parts." His opinion of himself,
in fact, steadily improved while he was in Germany. As he left the
country, he wrote that he would no longer imitate but henceforth
cultivate his own originality: "Let me then be Boswell."

This volume contains the valuable accounts of Boswell's interviews with Rousseau and Voltaire after he reached Switzerland.
Rather than use the note of introduction to Rousseau that Lord
Marishal had written for him, Boswell preferred his own, in which
he announced himself as an "ancient Scots gentleman of twenty-
four." After Rousseau's persecution for *Emile* and other works,
he, now in exile in Motiers, was perhaps at the height of his fame.
He was ill when Boswell arrived and said the interview would have
to be short, but Boswell stayed an hour and a half. They talked of
the Spanish and French characters, the union of Scotland and
England, the French invasion of Corsica, a Corsican constitution,
and other subjects. Boswell parted from Rousseau hoping that his
health would permit another interview. He had four more in the
next several days, despite Rousseau's telling him in the second one
that he, Boswell, was irksome and that he wanted him to leave.

The next time he saw Rousseau they discussed a sketch of
Boswell's life that he had sent to Rousseau,[16] in which he told of
the remorse he had suffered because of an intrigue with a married
woman whose father had been good to him. Rousseau advised him
to discontinue the relationship, since it was against his conscience.
On his fourth visit Boswell said he would leave only on condition
that Rousseau invite him to dinner the next day. It was agreed, and
in this last interview Rousseau was unusually gay. Boswell expressed
his disgust about the "shocking familiarity" of the Scots, and
Rousseau talked of the independence of cats and told Boswell that
Saint Paul, who was responsible for muddling Boswell's head,
would have been a good Anglican clergyman. When Boswell took
his leave, he and Rousseau were on the best of terms.

Boswell's experience with Voltaire, the French philosopher and
author, in Ferney, Switzerland, was also successful. He reached
Voltaire's handsome chateau armed with a letter of introduction
from Zelide's friend, Colonel Constant d'Hermenches. When
Boswell was ushered into an elegant room, Voltaire was annoyed

at being disturbed but came out wearing a blue dressing gown, received Boswell "with dignity," and sat erect. They talked about traveling in the Hebrides, about the difficulty of pronouncing English, and about the status of painting as an art in Scotland. Voltaire said it failed to flourish there, for an artist had to have warm feet.

Boswell asked Voltaire's neice, Mme Dennis, for permission to spend the night in the house so that he could the more conveniently see Voltaire. Voltaire replied to him with a gracious note, and Boswell was "very genteely" lodged in a room with a bed on which was spread a purple cloth lined with white quilted satin. During his visit, Boswell labored to convince Voltaire of the immortality of the soul. He sat by him and "touched the keys in unison with his imagination. I wish you could have heard the music," he wrote Temple. "He was all brilliance." Voltaire thought Shakespeare was a buffoon whom the English admired only because they had no taste; Addison was a great genius; but Johnson, "a superstitious dog." Two days later we find Boswell in Voltaire's dressing room, again trying to convince him that the soul was immortal. It is not on record that he succeeded.

The rest of Boswell's travels is recorded in the next Yale edition: *Boswell on the Grand Tour: Italy, Corsica, and France, 1765-1766*, edited by Frank Brady and Frederick A. Pottle (1955). This work is made up of Boswell's discontinuous Journal, memoranda and notes for his Journal, and many letters and miscellaneous documents. This phase of Boswell's life and journey could well be entitled "Boswell in Search of Love" (physical love, that is). He probably enjoyed more girls each week during the time encompassed by the volume than ever before or after. He declared, while in Rome, that after all, "one might allow one's self a little indulgence in a city where there are prostitutes licensed by the Cardinal Vicar." But with Italian women of fashion he had ill luck, though they were ready enough for a discreet tumble. He indicated reasons for his failure in a letter to Rousseau written nine months after he arrived in Italy. He entered the country too much like a penitent, with "ideas of the most rigorous morality"; and this attitude had made him proceed in his play with too much modesty. Accordingly, they "scorned his detours of delicacy," one lady frankly telling him he should go back to his books, for he knew too little of the world. When he was not too delicate, he was too blunt.

He never had known how to dissemble and use the subtle approach. In the process, however, he learned much. Italy, he informed Rousseau in a letter, did more for him than books could ever have done: it helped him correct his imagination.

This volume has a goodly share of high adventure, particularly when Boswell moves from one city to another. As he set out from Geneva, we see him jogging along through the Alps in a chaise and being carried over treacherous passages by an Alps "machine" consisting of two trees between which were twisted cords that served for a seat and back rest. Six men "changing two by two" carried him on this contrivance. They came to a grand prospect and then a plain on which stood a church with an "immensely ignorant" priest who lived like a hermit and provided mass for pilgrims. Traveling under the protection of the Dominican fathers, who gave him a letter of introduction for each place that he visited, Boswell proceeded on to Turin, where the Countess de St. Giles arranged for him to attend a public ball. He danced a minuet with the wife of the Spanish ambassador and tried much too indiscreetly to make love to the countess and other ladies. After reaching Parma, he began a close and salutary friendship with the scholar Alexandre Deleyre, a follower of Rousseau and the teacher of the duke of Parma's son.

In Rome, he began as part of his Journal (but did not get around to finishing it) a six-day "Course in Antiquities and the Arts," donned himself in silk for his presentation to the Pope, went to *conversationi* in palaces of Roman nobles, attended levees of cardinals, and became amazed at the scheming ambitions of church politicians. Also while there he met Lord Mounstuart, the earl of Bute's eldest son, who through a mutual friend arranged with Lord Auchinleck for Boswell to go with him on a tour of Italy. Accompanied by Lieutenant Colonel Edmonstone, who went along as a kind of "governor" for Mounstuart, and Paul Henry Mallett, Mounstuart's tutor in history, they visited a number of cities, ending up in Venice, where they separated amicably but under strained circumstances. Boswell, Mountstuart, and Mallet quarreled almost continuously, sometimes about nothing more important than where to stop next.

Boswell then proceeded to Florence and went forty miles out of the way to visit Virgil's home, about two miles from Mantua. He went from there to Siena, where he simultaneously pursued Porzia Sansedone and Girolama Piccolomini (or Moma). The story of his affairs with these ladies is one of the main strands of the action represented in the volume. Boswell sent his valet with a letter to one of them in his left pocket and a letter to the other one in his right pocket. After Boswell learned that Porzia conducted intrigues "according to the rules" but lacked warmth and sincerity, he abandoned his suit of her and concentrated on Moma, whose heart bled for him and continued to do so long after he left Italy, as was revealed in many letters included in the volume. As Moma's passion for him mounted, Boswell intensified the fervor of his pleas for Porzia's favors. Moma's only consolation during the years following Boswell's departure from Italy were an occasional letter from him and the sight of the little room where they had met secretly. Of all the women in Boswell's life save Mrs. Boswell, Moma was no doubt the one who loved him most.

Eventually, he began thinking seriously about finding a life-mate. This rather pleasant phase of his story is presented in *Boswell in Search of a Wife, 1766-1769,* edited by Frank Brady and Frederick A. Pottle (1956). When he returned to Auchinleck from his travels, the pastoral graces of the gardener's daughter, with whom he grew up, unexpectedly and suddenly put him in a delirium; but the thought of marrying beneath himself just as quickly brought him to sanity. His interest in the charming and sensible Miss Elizabeth Diana Bosville, whom he met in London, was also short-lived. He learned that she was engaged to another man before he got around to informing her of his interest in her. It was Boswell's connections with Mrs. Dodds ("Circe") and the Misses Blair, Boyd, and Montgomerie that give continuity and structure to the book, which consists mainly of his English and Scottish Journals, Journal memoranda and notes, parts of the manuscript for the *Life of Samuel Johnson,* and sundry letters.

While on a visit to Moffatt, according to a letter to Temple, Boswell found a "free" woman with whom to dally; for her husband was living with another woman. "Handsome, very lively, and admirably formed for amorous dalliance," Mrs. Dodds was kind, generous, and faithful; but she lacked good breeding and, as Boswell discovered, she had had other affairs. She moved to Edinburgh to be near him and eventually bore him a daughter. He made financial arrangements for them, and with the greatest of effort he broke away from Mrs. Dodds, but not for long. Eventually, though, he abandoned her.

Boswell rather seriously pursued the handsome, stately, and agreeable Miss Catherine Blair, a ward of his father who sat in their pew at church. Lord Auchinleck heartily approved of her, for her family were wealthy landholders. Not having been explicit about proposing, Boswell soon heard that she was engaged to a surgeon ("the Nabob") who had returned from India with accumulated wealth. When Boswell and the surgeon consulted each other about the matter, they discovered to their amusement that she was, in fact, engaged to another man.

In August, 1768, Boswell wrote Temple that, having escaped "the insensible Miss Blair and the furious Zelide," he was now captivated by Mary Ann Boyd of Ireland. She had a sweet countenance and was "formed like a Greecian nympth." When he went to Ireland to see her, he took along his cousin Margaret Montgomerie. Theirs was a perfect storybook situation; for, as they proceeded on their way, he told Margaret of his love for a woman other than Mary Ann. This other woman, he later informed her, was Margaret herself. In a letter to Temple he related with admirable restraint and sincerity the details of their beautiful but brief courtship. She was without dowry, however, and was therefore bitterly opposed by Boswell's father. Even greater was Boswell's opposition to his father's approaching second marriage. Both men were married the same day, November 19, 1769, and neither attended the ceremonies of the other. Lord Auchinleck married his cousin Elizabeth Boswell in Edinburgh, and his son and Margaret were married in Lainshaw, not far from Auchinleck. The relations between Boswell's family and his father and the new Lady Auchinleck were permanently cold and sometimes hostile.

Boswell was so occupied with his marriage and his law practice that he neglected his Journal during the first two years covered in the next Yale edition: *Boswell for the Defence, 1769-1774*, edited by William K. Wimsatt, Jr., and Frederick A. Pottle (1959). The editors filled in the gaps quite well, however, by utilizing, along with other documents, the correspondence of Boswell and Temple. We see Boswell busily engaged with criminal cases involving persons of low social status, which he sometimes handled mainly from a benevolent motive. Some of his clients were, for instance, two fifteen-year-old girls charged with the murder and robbery of a woman, a man who in a fit of anger stabbed his best friend, two tinkers who had burglarized a man's home and then fatally injured him, a schoolmaster charged with brutality and irregular attendance, and a man accused of stealing sheep. The last two cases occupied much labor on Boswell's part over a long period of time. John Hastie, the schoolmaster, whose case he pleaded in an appeal before the House of Lords, had won in the Scottish courts. When, therefore, Boswell took the stand, he knew that the lord chief justice was for reversal, so all that he hoped to do was make a good impression before Paoli, Oglethorpe, Garrick, and others who had come to hear him in his first appeal before the House of Lords. He was gratified by their expressions of approval.

The case of John Reid, the man accused of sheep stealing, occupies so many pages of the volume that at times it appears to be mainly Reid's story. At the trial in which Boswell received much applause for his "spirited" conduct of Reid's defense, Boswell's father was one of the judges whose vote for conviction prevailed; and a sentence of death was accordingly pronounced. Most of the Reid story, however, comes after the trial. Boswell went about having conferences with this person and that, hoping to find evidence of Reid's innocence so that the sentence of death could be changed to life imprisonment or transportation to the Colonies. His efforts failed, but the Reid story lingered on for many more pages; for Boswell made elaborate plans to recover the unfortunate man's body immediately after hanging in order to try reviving it. The project was not abandoned until almost the moment of execution, when Boswell was busily locating a house where an already engaged physician could work on the body. He gave up only after it was suggested that, in the event of success, he might be charged with postponing the transit of Reid's soul to heaven.

The story of himself that Boswell gives during the period covered in this volume, expecially after those first two rather serene years of 1769 and 1770, was characterized by restless activity in Edinburgh and London. He was ever aware of the worth of his "valuable" wife, but his frequent drinking and gambling led to shameful mistreatment of her. He spent much time in the company of fellow advocates in Edinburgh, but he detested their manners. On several trips to London he became increasingly involved in the life of the city. We see him attending a meeting of the managers of the *London Magazine*, of which he was one of the partners. He was so delighted with the "busy and bustling Countenances" of the other partners as the bells of St. Paul's struck the hours that he hugged himself in sheer delight. How different was the stimulating city scene. he commented, from "the usual objects of a Scots laird." He spent so much time with Johnson that late hours took a toll on his health. Ten years after meeting him, Boswell was a candidate for election to the famous Literary Club. He knew that one blackball would exclude him from it, and we see him one night anxiously awaiting the decision of the voting. He was admitted, of course. Johnson said no one would dare exclude him. It was about this time that Boswell announced to Johnson that he planned to write his life.

A dangerous period for Boswell is spelled out in the Journals and other papers that constitute Boswell: *The Ominous Years, 1774-1776* edited by Charles Ryskamp and Frederick A. Pottle (1963). Only four of the twenty months represent the combined duration of several trips to London, yet nearly a half of the book treats of these four months alone. Whatever the compensations, however genuine the pleasures that he experienced in Scotland (and there were certainly some), they never counterbalanced the frustrations he suffered because of protracted absences from London. Excessive drinking, gambling, and consorting with loose women and prostitutes all but ruined him. To compound his wretchedness, the lord justice clerk's son challenged him to a duel because of the insinuations against the lord justice clerk that had appeared in an article Boswell had written for the *London Chronicle*. He and Mrs. Boswell spent many sleepless nights in fear of the possible tragic outcome of the challenge. The matter was eventually cleared up, however, after Boswell in an interview with the irate son assured him he had meant no injury.

But Boswell does not present a sustained picture of wretchedness, and parts of his Journal are pleasant reading. We see him and his wife traveling by post-chaise to the nearby home of close friends and to the scenes of happy childhood experiences; enjoying hearty dinners with congenial and genteel friends and relatives; seeing a performance of *The Beggar's Opera* one night and *Hamlet* a few nights later. Boswell obviously enjoyed recounting such pleasant occasions, which, nevertheless, would sometimes be marred by sudden longing for English ideas and English ways of life. Perhaps nothing more was needed to set off this longing than the sight of Sir and Lady Oughton passing by on their way to the English Chapel.

Even as he left for one of his trips to London to talk with friends about getting called to the English bar, he told himself that "the Old Castle, the romantic rocks and woods of Auchinleck must never be forsaken." After he reached London, he called on Johnson, Beauclerk, and then Langton; dined with Paoli; went by to see Sir John Pringle, friend of his father and physician to the king and president of the Royal Society; and got a ticket for the next mayor's ball from John Wilkes, who had been reinstated in Parliament and was now lord mayor of London. No wonder Boswell wrote in his Journal many weeks later that he was unable to recall any part of his life that was flatter and more wretched than the two months since he returned to Scotland.

This volume contains one of Boswell's finest performances as a writer. It is his account of an interview with Mrs. Margaret Caroline Rudd, who is supposed to have descended from Scotch nobility. At seventeen she married a Lieutenant Rudd but very soon deserted him and began a life of pleasure. She had liaisons with wealthy men and then blackmailed them, served as governess in noble families, masqueraded as a countess, and forged bonds. Eventually apprehended, she spent six months in jail and stood trial; but, since the prosecution was ineffective and since her defense of her own case was unusually skillful, she was freed. Boswell stated that his curiosity to see this celebrated woman while in London led him to knock on her door in Westminster. From this point on, the story is so excellently told that, after completing it, we might well feel that we have been on the scene. We marvel not so much at Boswell's writing—and this reaction is proof of his genius—as at the consummate cleverness, really warm personality, and extraordinary charm of the remarkable woman whom he, along with himself, has truly brought to life.

Boswell gave a record of his life (mainly in Scottish and English Journals) for almost every day of the period covered in *Boswell in Extremes, 1776-1778*, edited by Charles McC. Weis and Frederick A. Pottle (1970). The title refers to what the editors in their introduction consider to be Boswell's tendency, especially at the time, of abruptly passing from ecstatic heights of bliss and glory to the depths of despair. His recklessness continued apace; once he got drunk enough to kiss a girl openly during burial services in a graveyard. On trips to Auchinleck and neighboring country seats, he sometimes enjoyed wholesome relief and short-lived return to calmness; but there was no gaiety. Back in

Edinburgh, he followed a monotonous, uneven, seldom pleasant course: he dined and strolled with his good friend Johnston, whose presence was comforting but seldom stimulating; attended Sunday morning and afternoon services with his father and accompanied him to dinner between services; argued with him about his own indebtedness and the question of entail (inheritance); had clandestine sex encounters, which he cryptically recorded in his Journal with Greek characters; dictated court arguments to his amanuensis; pleaded in court and between sessions; played whist with fellow lawyers; mourned the death of his son David and found much satisfaction in his little Veronica; experienced short periods of sobriety and good conversation; and irrevocably decided that there was no future, no dignity in his Court of Session career, and that he must therefore finally seek to enlarge his sphere in England.

This volume carries Boswell's record of his remarkable interview with the philosopher David Hume. He desperately needed to believe that death would not end his existence, and he just as desperately tried to convince himself that it would not. Could his beliefs withstand Hume's imperturbability in the very presence of death? He walked into Hume's drawing room and found the lean and ghastly appearing philosopher in a reclining position absorbed in the reading of Campbell's *Philosophy of Rhetoric*. When Boswell introduced the subject of religion and immortality, Hume denied belief in both. Boswell felt "a degree of horrour mixed with a sort of wild, strange, hurrying recollection" of his religious past. Through the whole ordeal he kept his faith; but the impressions that Hume made on him haunted him for a long time. There is a vivid, dramatic quality in Boswell's record of this interview that makes it good reading. The situation itself was quietly but intensely dramatic, and the sincerity of both men was unquestionable.

Many pages of this volume recount Boswell's pleasant jaunt to Ashbourne and an extended visit there with Johnson, as well as a long stay in London, when he spent some of his happiest times with him and the men of his group. When Boswell subsequently prepared copy for the *Life of Samuel Johnson*, he made use of these pages from his Journal. While in London he added two more names to the already impressive list of persons he had interviewed. One of the interviews was with General John Burgoyne, who back in London after his surrender to the Americans at Saratoga, was soon to take the stand for a parliamentary investigation. Boswell did not record this interview in his Journal but gave an account of it in a letter to Temple which unfortunately is not among the Temple letters that were recovered. We know of this interview, therefore, only through a number of significant references to it.

The other interview was with the distinguished Scot, the earl of Marchmont, lord keeper of the Great Seal of Scotland, intimate friend of Alexander Pope and Lord Bolinbroke, and author and politician whose Deistic ideas influenced Pope in his *Essay on Man*. Boswell's long conversation with Lord Marchmont provides intimate sidelights on Pope's physical appearance and personality, as well as interesting anecdotes about Bolingbroke. Pope's body, we are reminded, was bent and crooked; and we learn that he required sleep before and after dinner. His conversation was vivacious as long as he lead it; otherwise, he invariably fell asleep. He was loyal to the Roman Catholic Church but had long since become unsettled in his faith and inactive in attendance at mass. He was haphazard in keeping his accounts, failing to separate received from paid sums. As for Bolinbroke, his conversation improved with wine, Marchmont reported; in fact, he would drink and hunt with him just to hear him talk.

The last Journal in the volume now under consideration, *Boswell in Extremes*, ends in May, 1778; and Boswell died six years later. Some of the remaining Journals and other documents, which will eventually be published in the Yale trade editions, are privately printed in *The Private Papers of James Boswell* (XIII-XVIII). They depict no substantial change in Boswell's way of life, and they are written with the same unabashed fidelity to truth, whether pretty or ugly, and with the same childlike intensity during the ever decreasing moments when he wanted to hug himself for the sheer joy of being alive in London.

We witness the sad and wretched spectacle of Boswell at his father's deathbed when Lady Auchinleck refused him access to the sick man and he stood off and wept. As he accompanied his father's body for interment in the family vault, he felt that he himself was being taken to his own execution. During intervals between gaming, drinking, and running after girls, he managed to plead his law cases with ease and force; and, as the new laird of Auchinleck, he tried but failed to do his duty to his tenants and to his ancestral estate. He entertained such a variety of people at Auchinleck that he had to keep his accounts in a Book of Company and Liquors. Absent from London at the time of Johnson's death, he was "stunned, and in a kind of maze" when he heard of it.

Boswell's Journals still report activities of the Literary Club at which he was a regular attendant when in London. He spent as much time as ever with the wits of Johnson's circle, but his interest in reporting their conversation gradually diminished. He was often with Malone, who assisted him in getting first the Hebrides Journal off to the publishers and then the *Life*. On one of several occasions when he talked intimately with the king at levees at the Court of St. James, His Majesty told Boswell that there would be many foolish lives of Johnson written but that he wanted Boswell to make his the best since he had known Johnson "more intimately than any other man." Many entries in the Journal tell of Boswell's horrifying expectation of a duel with Lord Alexander Macdonald, who was offended because of derogatory remarks made about him in *The Journal of a Tour to the Hebrides*. When Boswell was admitted to the English bar, he gave an absorbing description of the induction formalities and the inauguration dinner. He told of bringing his wife and children to live with him in the English capital and then of taking Mrs. Boswell back to Scotland after he had failed as a London lawyer. He was vexed that he could not "unite Auchinleck and London," but he continued to indulge the hope that it might yet be possible.

He reported on the success of the *Life of Samuel Johnson* and the dinner he gave to celebrate it. Miserably lonesome after Reynold's death, he could not have returned to Scotland had he wanted to: for his addiction to English ways of living doomed him to continued failure in London. After dining at Malone's with Langton and Courtenay, he wrote in his Journal: "I have lost the faculty of recording conversation. Or perhaps I have seen and heard so much now that no conversation impresses me much." His last Journal entry was April 12, 1794, thirteen months before his death. His Journal did indeed, as he said it would, "afford materials for a very curious narrative."

CHAPTER 9

Boswell's Significance

T HE name *Boswell* is seldom mentioned without the words
and Johnson coming to mind, for James Boswell is hardly
thought of as an author who had a literary career of his own. Yet
when Benjamin Franklin, General Oglethorpe, and Dr. Johnson
went to his quarters that day in 1768 to pay respects to the author
of *An Account of Corsica*, just then published, he was already a
minor celebrity and only twenty-eight years old. This incident
occurred twenty-three years before he published the biography that
made him famous and firmly established for posterity a preeminent
place for its subject among the engaging personalities of all time.

Known in 1768 almost solely for the book on Corsica and for some
rather amazing publicity stunts in the furtherance of the cause of
Corsican independence, he had previously tried his hand at literary
and dramatic criticism, poetry, and short fiction. And he had already
written some of the best parts of the Journal that was to remain his
chief occupation for virtually the rest of his life. Two series of
periodical essays, a few political pamphlets, and many miscellaneous
items round out the career of an author who until recently was
known chiefly for his two books about Johnson— *The Journal of a
Tour to the Hebrides* and *The Life of Samuel Johnson, LL.D.*

Boswell's stock has gradually risen since persistent searching in
our century and the necessary capital brought to light an un-
precedented mass of hidden material. The Boswell papers have
provided the evidence that was needed to reexamine Boswell's
biographical art and to understand better the creative process that
produced the great *Life*. They also brought to the fore his pre-
eminence in the area of autobiographical writing; and, through the
gradual publication of the Journals and other personal documents
in accessible trade editions, he has recently come to be popularly
known as a journal writer of great merit, thanks to the editors of the
Yale editions of the Private Papers.

Not all who have assessed Boswell's works have, either before or after the discovery of his papers, properly assessed him. The powerful rhetoric of Thomas Babington Macaulay, writing a century before their discovery, popularized Boswell as a man of puny intellect—as a fool who somehow wrote a great book by accident and not through the operation of intellect or imagination.[1] This estimate was unwarranted by even the limited evidence within Macaulay's reach. All the more unjust is the image brought forward by C. E. Vulliamy, who wrote after libraries began receiving limited editions of many of the Journals and other papers; for he beheld a Boswell still more contemptible than the effigy fashioned by Macaualy's deft hands.[2] Lytton Strachey viewed him in a similar light;[3] and, while Harold Nicolson[4] and Hesketh Pearson[5] gave some recognition to his art, their conclusions suggest limited use of available documents.

Conversely, there are those who recognized Boswell's artistic merits long before discovery of the Boswell Papers. Robert Anderson, who published a biography of Johnson only four years after Boswell's appeared, praised Boswell for his intellectual powers, his ability to observe human life justly, his strength of mind, his abundance of knowledge, his picturesque imagination, his turn for poetry, and his humor and wit.[6] George Mallory, Chauncey Brewster Tinker, and Walter Raleigh, all writing before 1915,[7] also presented incisive observations about Johnson's biographer. To be sure, there is much that these writers were unable to see and some of their conjectures needed substantiation from evidence yet to be provided by the Journals.

Boswell was not the kind of biographer that can be successfully imitated. Yet, as he sought to adhere to the truth—even if he never intended to present all of it—and as he refused either to eugolize or to defame, he established the standard for excellent biography. It was not chiefly in his regard for truth, however, that he influenced biography in the nineteenth century; instead, it was in the nineteenth-century view of the *Life of Samuel Johnson* as a specimen of that form of expression which was a major feature of romanticism. According to this view, Boswell's experience and his knowledge of Johnson were dominated by his inner self; in other words, he knew Johnson by knowing himself in Johnson.[8] Thus the biography, as André Maurois says of art, was a means of expression, a "deliverance."[9] In calling attention to this side of Boswell's art, Thomas

Carlyle helped to establish him as a force in the development of romantic biography. He interpreted Boswell's regard for Johnson not as "sychophancy, which is the lowest, but Reverence, which is the highest of human feelings."[10]

Boswell's influence on nineteenth-century biography was thus active and organic in the practice and theory of life-writing. In our own time, on the other hand, its position is that of a splendid success against which the success of any other biography must inevitably be measured. The modern biographer is no more opposed to denigration or uncritical praise, no less concerned with the truth than Boswell was; but his search for truth involves probings into the subconscious mind and into doubts, uncertainties, and complexities of the conscious mind. These aims were not encompassed in Boswell's quest for truth, which, after all, he was able to pursue only within limits made possible by the scholarship and knowledge of his day. An increased awareness of the complexity and the mobility of human beings and a greater sense of their disunity have lead modern psychologists and philosophers to investigations of the "divided soul."

These investigations have enlarged the modern biographer's view of human personality. According to Maurois,[11] it is the nature of their search and the methods which they employ that differentiate their work from Boswell's. Maurois might have noticed that, while Boswell's representation of Johnson did not involve the modern biographer's broadened and deepened view of personality, hardly a day passed without his revealing in his Journal either a brief or sustained effort on his part to probe into the mysteries of his own consciousness. Countless discriptions of his mental states should have unique value for psychologists who wish to investigate the roots of his incredible behavior.

Boswell cannot be called an autobiographer in the true sense of the word. Except for the brief *Memoirs* that he sent to the *London Magazine,* he did not write a connected story of his life. He was essentially a diarist, a keeper of a journal. Yet, as Donald A. Stauffer has noticed, "No one, in any age or nation, has left such a complete and satisfactory record of his own life as Boswell."[12] This voluminous record is mainly in the form of journals covering most of his adult life, but it also includes thousands of letters which he received and carefully preserved. Furthermore, he asked his correspondents to return his own letters to him; he got many of them back and added them to his vast collection of personal papers. Thus he assiduously gathered together materials for his biography-auto-biography that is now being written and compiled at Yale University. Whether we term Boswell a diarist or an autobiographer, he has left to posterity a unique record of a life, some portions of which have solid literary merit. Although, as we have noted, the Boswell that emerges at the beginning of the Journal is about the same one that we find at the end, our knowledge of him is fuller and our estimate, therefore, sounder.

So copious are the autobiographical materials in the books and articles that Boswell published in his own time that Percy Fitz-gerald, writing his biography near the end of the nineteenth cen-tury and long before the Journals came to light, thought that they were uncommonly abundant. Yet, curiously enough, almost no one except Stauffer and the Yale editors have perceived the importance of this phase of Boswell's writings; it has been virtually unnoticed by writers dealing specifically with autobiography.[13] None of the surprisingly few full-length biographies of Boswell,[14] except Fitz-gerald's, considered it important enough to discuss.

Boswell's admiration for English ways wielded a potent and de-cisive influence on his literary career and thus rendered him emi-nently fit to reflect the social, literary, and aesthetic milieu in which he flourished. The England of his day had not yet achieved economic, social, and political stability. Politics was not without corruption, the religious question was not fully settled, and the industrial revolution was creating grave social problems; but the nation was gradually gaining a sure footing and would soon view with pride its internal strength by comparison with the unsettled conditions in revolutionary France. It was a century that Leslie Stephens chose to characterize not by its negative qualities but by its sound common sense, its increased toleration, and its social and industrial advancement.[15]

This state of affairs seems to have been reflected in the sense of well-being and sane optimism that, by and large, pervaded the political and literary circles among which Boswell and Johnson moved. It, was, in fact, the tone of Johnson's famous Literary Club, which, in its distinguished membership, embraced science, reli-gion, art, music, the theater, politics, and literature. It is partly as a reflection of the literary ideas and wider interests of this group, which cultivated conversation as an art, that we value Boswell. In

his genuine delight in the pleasures of wit and conversation he fig-
ured typically as an eighteenth-century man of letters; and here we
might find the geatest single source of his success as Johnson's
biographer.

He had a deep-rooted respect for authority, and he often gave oral
and written expression to his approval of the ancients as critics and
as arbiters of taste. In his verse, which seldom achieved a fair competence and never rose above it, he was often guilty of the worst
excesses of poetic diction; but in his prose he emulated with some
success Addison's ease and lucidity. His ideas concerning inspiration and enthusiasm betrayed the faults which the neoclassicists
sought to correct, but the restraint which the tastes of the time de-
manded curbed his impulses when the occasion required decorum,
and it influenced his prose style.

Soon after Boswell settled in London and "plunged into the wide
speculative scene of English ambition," he complained to Malone
of his failure as a London lawyer. Malone replied that he probably
could have succeeded at the English bar but chose instead "a wide
and varied course of life." Malone was one of Boswell's wisest
and best friends, and his comment seems to imply that only from
Boswell's failure in London could come the great success for which
posterity would know him. Only in London could he have wrought
the work that Burke thought was a greater monument to Johnson's
fame than all of Johnson's works put together[16] and that Carlyle
rated higher than any other book of the eighteenth century.[17]

The uniqueness of this contribution is the deliberate fusing of
Boswell's own life story, his own experiences, with Johnson's story.
The coalescence of ordinary experience with artistic achievement
seems in his case to have been exceptional. Elements in and outside
Britian to which he was exposed and which attracted his attention
permeated his mind and art and nourished his peculiar genius. At
no stage in his adult life did he ever seem to be unconscious of this
fact. Ever aware of the enrichment which his wide experiences and
interests would inevitably bestow upon his biographical work, he
seems to have sought out experiences and to have cultivated interests for the sake of the monumental *Life of Samuel Johnson* to
which he had committed himself. He can thus be said to have planned much of his life deliberately out of considerations primarily
artistic.

Notes and References

Chapter One

1. *The Private Papers of James Boswell from Malahide Castle*, 18 vols., eds. Geoffrey Scott and Frederick A. Pottle, (New York, 1928-33), II, 189.
2. *Ibid.*, XVII, 101.
3. *Ibid.*, VII, 42; X, 181.
4. *Boswell for the Defence, 1769-1774*, eds. William K. Wimsatt and Frederick A. Pottle (New York, 1957), p. 185.
5. *Boswell: The Ominous Years, 1774-1776*, eds. Charles Ryskamp and Frederick A. Pottle (New York, 1963), pp. 1, 86.
6. Private Papers, IV, 61.
7. *London Journal, 1762-1763*, ed. Frederick A. Pottle (New York, 1950).
8. Albert Britt, *The Great Biographers* (New York, 1936), p. 71.
9. *Letters of James Boswell*, 2 vols., ed. Chauncey Brewster Tinker (Oxford, 1924), I, 8.

Chapter Two

1. *Letters*, I, 2.
2. *Scots Magazine*, XX (August, 1758), 420. Reprinted in *A Collection of Original Poems by Scotch Gentlemen* (Edinburgh, 1762), II, 68.
3. Frederick A. Pottle, *The Literary Career of James Boswell, Esq.* (Oxford, 1929), p. 216, concluded that this must be Boswell's essay. It was published in the *Scots Magazine*, XX (December, 1758), 624.
4. *London Journal*, p. 6.
5. *Ibid.*, p. 5.
6. Quoted by Andrew G. Hoover, "Boswell's First London Visit," *Virginia Quarterly Review*, XXX (1953), 246.
7. Frederick A. Pottle, "Bozzy and Yorick," *Blackwood's Magazine*, CCXVII (March, 1925), 298-313.
8. *Scots Magazine*, XXIII (September, 1761), 469-71.
9. Private Papers, I, 127.
10. James Boswell, *The Hypochondriack*, 2 vols., ed. Margery Bailey (Stanford, 1928), I, 53.

11. *Ibid.*, II, 12.

12. This self-criticism Boswell scribbled in a copy of the *Observations* at one time preserved in the Auchinleck library, according to Pottle, *Literary Career of James Boswell*, p. 5.

13. Leslie Stephen, *The History of English Thought in the Eighteenth Century*, 2 vols. (London, 1902), II, 389.

14. Quoted by Pottle, *Literary Career of James Boswell*, p. 5.

15. James Boswell, *The Life of Samuel Johnson*, 6 vols., ed. G. B. Hill; revised, L. F. Powell (Oxford, 1934-50), I, 459.

16. *Letters*, I, viii.

17. Private Papers, XVIII, 81-82.

18. *Ibid.*, IV, 120-21.

19. *Boswell in Holland, 1763-1764*, ed. Frederick A. Pottle (New York, 1952); *Boswell on the Grand Tour: Germany and Switzerland 1764*, ed. Frederick A. Pottle (New York, 1953); *Boswell on the Grand Tour: Italy, Corsica, and France, 1765-1766*, eds. Frank Brady and Frederick A. Pottle (New York, 1955).

20. Private Papers, VII, 70.

21. Facts about the case were obtained principally from Boswell's publications mentioned here and from Walter Lowry, "James Boswell, Scots Advocate and English Barrister, 1740-1795," *Stanford Law Review*, II (1950), 471-95.

22. *Letters*, II, 96.

23. *Memoirs of James Boswell, Esq.* printed in *European Magazine*, IX (May, 1791), 325-26. Reprinted in Frederick A. Pottle, *Literary Career of James Boswell* (Oxford, 1929), pp. xxix-xliv.

24. *Ibid.*, p. 326.

25. *Scots Magazine*, XXIX (July, 1767), 337; (December), 621, 630, 702; XXX (November, 1768), 855. By examining Boswell's own marked file of the *London Chronical* for 1767-75, Professor Pottle discovered many more amazing facts about Boswell's journalistic activities in connection with the Douglas cause as well as the Corsican situation. See his "The Incredible Boswell," *Blackwood's Magazine*, CCXVIII (August, 1925), 149-65.

26. *Ibid.*, XXX (July, August, October, 1768), 347, 410, 539.

27. *Ibid.*, 511, 545.

Chapter Three

1. James Boswell, *An Account of Corsica, The Journal of a Tour to that Island; and the Memoirs of Pascal Paoli* (London, 1768), p. 272.

2. Jean Jacques Rousseau, *Social Contract* (Oxford, 1953), Bk. II, p. 308.

3. Pottle, "The Incredible Boswell," p. 149.

4. *Scots Magazine*, XXIX (April, 1767), 214.

5. The first two editions were published in 1768 in Glasgow and London,

respectively; the third, in London in 1769. These comprised both the *Account* and the *Tour*. The latter was published separately in the following editions: ed. G. B. Hill, along with the Erskine Correspondence (London, 1879); ed. S. C. Roberts (Cambridge, 1923); ed. Morchard Bishop (London, 1951). The *Tour* was reprinted in *Boswell on the Grand Tour: Italy, Corsica, and France, 1765-66*, eds. Frank Brady and Frederick A. Pottle (New York) 1956), and in Moray McLaren, *Corsica Boswell: Paoli, Johnson and Freedom (London, 1966)*.

6. *Life of Johnson*, II, 70.

7. *Boswelliana*, ed. Charles Rogers (London, 1874), p. 299.

8. *Scots Magazine*, XXX (September, 1769), 453.

9. *British Essays in Favour of the Brave Corsicans* (London, 1769), pp. v-xii. Professor Pottle thinks Boswell also wrote Essays VI, XII, and XLV (*Literary Career of James Boswell*, pp. 81-83).

Chapter Four

1. In 1771 Boswell wrote to Garrick of his having "some concern" in this periodical. *Letters*, I, p. 183. In 1775 he informed Temple that he was "a proprietor" of it. *Ibid*, 217.

2. *London Magazine*, XXXIX (August, September, October, 1770), 397-98; 468-71; 513-17.

3. *London Journal*, p. 5.

4. Private Papers, VIII, 103.

5. *The Works of Shakespeare. In which the Beauties Observed by Pope, Warburton, and Dodd are pointed out*. 8 vols. (Edinburgh, 1771).

6. *London Magazine*, XVI-LXX (October, 1777—August, 1783). Boswell also sent articles to *The Public Advertiser* under the name "Rampager." They have not been available for consideration here. See *Boswell for the Defense*, p. 172, n. 7; p. 279.

7. Margery Bailey, ed. *Boswell's Column* (The "Hypochondriack" papers) (London, 1951), pp. xiif.

8. Private Papers, I, 56.

9. *Ibid*.

10. "Hypochondriack," I, 121-22. (See above, note 10, Chapter 2.)

11. *Scots Magazine*, XXXIV (April, 1772), 187-96, 225-32.

12. *Gentleman's Magazine*, Vol. LV (May, 1785), Part I, p. 359.

Chapter Five

1. *Memoirs*, XIX, 407.

2. *Ibid*.

3. *Journal of a Tour to the Hebrides* (Volume V of the Hill-Powell *Life*), p. 78, n. 5. Excepting in Note 8, all references to the *Tour* in this chapter

will be to this edition.

4. *Letters of James Boswell*, ed. C. B. Tinker, 2 vols. (Oxford, 1924), I, 222.

5. *Tour*, p. 182.

6. Samuel Johnson, *A Journey to the Western Islands of Scotland*, ed. R. W. Chapman (Oxford, 1924), p. 11.

7. *Tour*, p. 77.

8. *Tour*, ed. Frederick A. Pottle and Charles H. Bennett (New York, 1936), pp. x-xiii and *passim*.

9. *Tour*, pp. v-viii. This and remaining references to the *Tour* are from the Hill-Powell edition of the *Life*, Vol. V.

10. Private Papers, XIV, 197.

11. *Ibid.*, VI, 169-70.

12. *Ibid.*, 98.

13. *Ibid.*, XVI, 82.

14. *Tour*, p. 1.

15. *Ibid.*, p. 145, n. 2. See also *Gentleman's Magazine*, Vol LVI, Part I (April, 1786), p. 285.

16. *Gentleman's Magazine*, Vol. LVI, Part I (April, 1786), p. 285.

17. Private Papers, XII, 138-45, *passim*; 221-59, *passim*.

18. *Tour*, p. 2.

19. Percy H. Fitzgerald, *The Life of James Boswell*, 2 vols. (New York, 1891), II, 47.

20. *Ibid.*, II, 59.

21. Hester Lynch Thrale (later Piozzi), *Letters to the Late Samuel Johnson, LL.D.*, 2 vols. (London, 1788).

22. Private Papers, XVII, 74-75.

23. Pottle, *Literary Career of James Boswell*, pp. 131-32.

24. Fitzgerald, *The Life of James Boswell*, II, pp. 104-5.

25. Private Papers, XVII, 57.

26. *Ibid.*, XVII, 29.

27. *Ibid.*, XVII, 96-97.

28. *Ibid.*

29. *Scots Magazine*, XLVIII (April, 1786), 178.

30. *Gentleman's Magazine*, Vol. LVI, Part I (March, 1786), pp. 237-40.

31. *Scots Magazine*, Appendix, LII (1790), 625.

32. *Gentleman's Magazine*, LVI (August, 1786).

33. *Ibid.*, Vol. LXI, Part I (April, 1791), 367, 564.

34. *Scots Magazine*, LIV (May, 1791), 243.

35. This explanation is given by Professor Pottle, *Literary Career of James Boswell*, pp. 137-41.

36. *Memoirs*, XXX, 323-26; 404-7.

37. *Letters*, II, pp. 407 *et seq*.

Chapter Six

1. Sir John Hawkins, *The Life of Samuel Johnson, LL.D.* (London, 1787).

2. *Life of Johnson*, I, 25. This and all other quotations are from the George Birkbeck Hill edition, revised and enlarged by L. F. Powell, 6 vols. (Oxford, 1934-50).

3. Volume VI of the Private Papers (*The Making of the Life of Johnson*).

4. Frances Burney (Madame d'Arblay), *Diary and Letters of*, edited by her niece, 7 vols. (London, 1813-46).

5. Boswell appears here (as he wrote "in a work much in vogue at this time") to have been referring to the *Decline*, for Hume had complimented Gibbon on it two days earlier. *Life of Johnson*, Vol. II, p. 512, n. 5.

6. Boswell, *Journal of a Tour to the Hebrides* (London, 1785) and Johnson, *Journey to the Western Islands of Scotland* (London, 1775).

7. *Journal of a Tour to the Hebrides*, ed. Frederick A. Pottle and Charles H. Bennett (New York, 1936), p. 291.

8. *Life of Johnson*, III, 79.

9. *Ibid.*, IV, 108.

Chapter Seven

1. Noticed by Donald A. Stauffer, *The Art of Biography in Eighteenth Century England* (Princeton, 1941), p. 447.

2. See Bertram Davis's introduction to his abridged edition of *The Life of Samuel Johnson, LL.D.* by Sir John Hawkins (New York, 1961).

3. P. A. W. Collins, "Boswell's Contacts with Johnson," *Notes and Queries*, April, 1956 (Vol. CCI of the continuous series); *Life of Johnson*, Vol. I, p. 11, n. 2.

4. Thomas Babington Macaulay, review of Croker's edition of the *Life of Johnson*, *Miscellaneous Works of Lord Macaulay*, ed. Lady Trevelyan, 5 vols. (New York, 1880), I, 581.

5. Advertisement to the second edition of the *Life of Johnson*, quoted in Hill-Powell edition, I, 11.

6. *Life of Johnson*, V, 415.

7. *Ibid.*, 414.

8. Private Papers, XVIII, 122-23.

9. Advertisement to the Second Edition of the *Life of Johnson*, Hill-Powell edition, I, 10.

10. This is shown by Geoffrey Scott in a special volume, Volume VI, of the Private Papers of James Boswell, *The Making of the Life of Johnson*; also Volume 2, Yale Research Edition of the Private Papers of James Boswell: *The Correspondence and Other Papers of James Boswell Relating to the Making of the Life of Johnson*, edited by Marshall Waingrow (New York, 1970), pp. xxlf.

11. *Letters of James Boswell to the Rev. W. J. Temple*, ed. Thomas Seccombe (London, 1908), p. 218.

12. Reprinted in *Life of Johnson*, I, lxvii.

13. See above, p. 62.

14. *Life of Johnson*, III, pp. 427-32.

15. See above, pp. 94-95.

16. *Memoirs of James Boswell, Esq. European Magazine* (May, 1791), p. 324.

17. *Boswell's Column (The Hypochondriack)*, ed. Margery Bailey (London, 1951), p. 357.

18. *Journal of a Tour to the Hebrides*, ed. Frederick A. Pottle and Charles H. Bennett (New York, 1936), p. 379, n. 3.

19. *Life of Johnson*, II, 49.

20. *The Hypochondriack*, I, 140.

21. *Gentleman's Magazine*, Vol. LVII, Part I (1792), 18.

22. *Ibid.*, LXIVI (1794), 32-34.

23. *Ibid.*, 1009.

24. Private Papers, XVIII, 278.

Chapter Eight

1. *The Private Papers of James Boswell from Malahide Castle*, 18 vols. Geoffrey Scott, editor, Vols. I-VI; Frederick A. Pottle, editor, Vols. VII-XVIII; privately printed (New York, 1928-33).

2. In his review of Vulliamy's *James Boswell*, *Nation* (April 5, 1933), 136-37.

3. See below, pp. 169-70.

4. *Memoirs*, XIX, 323-26; 404-7.

5. Published for the first time in Frederick A. Pottle, *James Boswell: The Earlier Years, 1740-1769* (New York, 1966), pp. 1-7.

6. See especially *Letters of James Boswell*, edited by C. B. Tinker, 2 vols. (Oxford, 1924), and *Letters of James Boswell Addressed to the Rev. W. J. Temple*, edited by Thomas Seccombe (London, 1908).

7. Private Papers, XVIIi, 192.

8. Quoted in Chauncey Brewster Tinker, *Young Boswell* (Boston, 1922), p. 192.

9. *Letters*, II, 372.

10. *London Journal*, pp. 39-40.

11. This idea is developed by Roy Pascal, *Design and Truth in Autobiography* (Cambridge, 1960).

12. *Journal of a Tour to the Hebrides* (Vol. V of the *Life of Johnson*), p. 52.

13. Private Papers, I, 55-138. The jaunt began September 14, 1762, and ended November 14.

14. See above, p. 91.

15. See above, pp. 28-33.

16. See above, pp. 141-142.

Chapter Nine

1. Thomas Babington Macaulay, Review of Croker's edition of Boswell's *Life of Johnson*, *The Edinburgh Review*, LIV (September, 1831), 1-38; "Essay on Johnson," *Encyclopaedia Britannica*, 1856.

2. C. E. Vulliamy, *James Boswell* (New York, 1933), *passim*.

3. Lytton Strachey, *Portraits in Miniature and Other Essays* (London, 1931), pp. 87-97.

4. Harold Nicolson, *The Development of English Biography* (London, 1933), pp. 87-108.

5. Hesketh Pearson, *Johnson and Boswell—the Story of Their Lives* (New York, 1959), *passim*.

6. Robert Anderson, *The Life of Samuel Johnson, LL.D.* (London, 1795).

7. George Mallory, *Boswell the Biographer* (London, 1912); Chauncey Brewster Tinker, *Young Boswell* (Boston, 1922); Walter Raleigh, *Six Essays on Johnson* (Oxford, 1910), pp. 9-12 and *passim*.

8. Francis R. Hart, "Boswell and the Romantics: A Chapter in the History of Biographical Theory," *Journal of English Literary History*, XXVII (1960), 61.

9. Andre Maurois, *Aspects of Biography* (Cambridge, 1929), p. 60.

10. Thomas Carlyle, "Boswell's *Life of Johnson*," in *Critical and Miscellaneous Essays*, Collected and Republished, four vols. in two (London, 1888), II, 60.

11. *Memoirs*, p. 182.

12. Donald A. Stauffer, *The Art of Biography in Eighteenth Century England* (Princeton, 1941), p. 412.

13. Wayne Schumaker, *English Autobiography: Its Emergence, Materials and Forms* (University of California Press, 1954); E. Stuart Bates, *Inside Out: An Introduction to Autobiography* (Oxford, 1936); Roy Pascal, *Design in Autobiography* (Cambridge, 1960); H. N. Wethered, *The Curious Art of Autobiography* (New York, 1956), p. 2.

14. Percy H. Fitzgerald, *The Life of James Boswell*, 2 vols. (New York, 1891); Wyndham Lewis, *James Boswell, a Short Life* (London, 1952); W. Keith Leask, *James Boswell* (New York, 1896); C. E. Vulliamy, *James Boswell* (New York, 1933).

15. Stephen, *The History of English Thought in the Eighteenth Century*, Vol. I. p. 389.

16. Quoted by Powell, *Life of Johnson*, I, 10.

17. *Ibid*.

Selected Bibliography

PRIMARY SOURCES

Professor Pottle's exhaustive 335-page bibliography of Boswell's writings (*The Literary Career of James Boswell*) at first might give the impression that, prolific as Boswell was he produced ten times as much as he actually did. It comprises more than three hundred entries, and about a hundred of these are books and pamphlets; the remainder are poems, essays, and miscellaneous short items in periodicals, newspapers, and broadsides. Our view of what Boswell really did write must shrink, then, when we realize that many of these entries are for further editions or printings, or for translations by other hands.

For example, there are six entries for *Dorando*; twenty-one for *An Account of Corsica*; fourteen for the *Journal of a Tour to the Hebrides*; and thirty-five for the *Life of Samuel Johnson*, which include German and Russian abridgments, and various editions not prepared by Boswell himself. Furthermore, Boswell's connections with certain other items are scant indeed. If, for example, it were certain that he edited *The Letters of Lady Jane Douglas* (of which there were two editions), his part in the book would still be limited to only a few introductory statements; and six other works listed were only published or edited by Boswell. Indeed, after we take into account these facts, the list of his publications is small (merely about thirty; and, of that number, there are only three full-length books, the remainder being pamphlets, broadsides, or single poems). What he sent to periodicals and newspapers further swells the list of his writings, for he doubtless had a healthy appetite for a look at his scribblings, signed or unsigned, in the columns of magazines and newspapers. What is given in the following bibliography constitutes the bulk of his contributions to periodicals, for countless other items are too slight to deserve listing.

1. *Separate Publications by Boswell* (This part of the bibliography is hardly selective, for it contains very nearly every item that Boswell published separately; that is, those not appearing exclusively or at all in magazines or newspapers.)

Observations, Good or Bad, Stupid or Clever, Serious or Jocund on Squire Foote's Dramatic Entertainment, entitled, The Minor. By a Genius.

Edinburg: n.p., 1760. (Boswell later repudiated this foolish imitation of Sterne.)

An Elegy on the Death of an Amiable Young Lady with an Epistle from Manalcas to Lycidas, to which are prefixed Three Critical Recommendatory Letters. Edinburgh: Alexander Donaldson, 1761. (Two poems by Boswell and three critical letters about them—one by himself and the other two by Andrew Erskine and George Dempster, respectively.)

An Ode to Tragedy. Edinburgh: Alexander Donaldson, 1761. (Title page carries the pseudonym "A Gentleman from Scotland.")

The Cub at New-Market: A Tale. London: R. and J. Dodsley, 1762. (A poem in doggerel.)

A Collection of Original Poems by Scotch Gentlemen. 2 vols. Edinburgh: Alexander Donaldson, 1762. Volume II. (Boswell helped to compile this volume and was one of its largest contributors.)

Critical Strictures on the New Tragedy of Elvira Written by David Malloch. London: W. Flexney, 1763. (Coauthor with Andrew Erskine and George Demster.)

Letters between The Honourable Andrew Erskine, and James Boswell, Esq. London: W. Flexney, 1763. (This is the first item appearing with Boswell's name on the title page.) These letters were also published with *The Journal of a Tour to Corsica,* ed. George Birkbeck Hill, London: De La Rue & Co., 1789; and selections from this correspondence were subjoined to Thomas Seccombe's edition of *Boswell's Letters to* Temple, London: Sidgwick & Jackson, 1908.

Disputatio Juridica. Edinburgh: n.p., 1766. (A thesis that Boswell submitted in completion of his law studies.)

The Douglas Cause. (A poem in the form of a broadside.) Edinburgh: n.p., 1767.

Dorando, A Spanish Tale. London: J. Wilkie, 1767. (A prose allegorical treatment of the Douglas case.) Modern edition, London: Mathews and Marrot, 1930.

The Essence of the Douglas Cause. London: J. Wilkie, 1767. (An industrious compilation of arguments and proofs, only the advertisement of which was written by Boswell.)

Letters of the Right Honourable Lady Jane Douglas. London: J. Wilkie, 1767. (Boswell is thought to be one of seven editors.)

An Account of Corsica, The Journal of a Tour to that Island; and the Memoirs of Pascal Paoli. Glasgow: Edward and Charles Dilly, 1768. (The second edition was published in London the same year and the third the next year. These comprised both the *Account* and the *Tour.* The latter has been published separately in the following editions: ed. G. B. Hill, along with the Erskine Correspondence, London: Thomas De la Rue and Co., 1879; ed. S. C. Roberts, Cambridge: Clarendon Press,

1923; ed. Morchard Bishop, London: Williams and Norgate, 1951. It was also reprinted in *Boswell on the Grand Tour: Italy, Corsica, and France, 1765-1766*, eds. Frank Brady and F. A. Pottle, New York: McGraw-Hill, 1956, and Moray McLaren, *Corsica Boswell: Paoli, Johnson and Freedom*, London: Secker and Warburg, 1966.)

British Essays in Favour of the Brave Corsicans. London: Edward and Charles Dilly, 1769. (Boswell wrote only the Preface and probably three of the essays.)

Verses in the Character of a Corsican at Shakespeare's Jubilee, At Stratford-upon-Avon, Sept. 6, 1769. By James Boswell, Esq. (A broadside.) Stratford: n.p., 1769.

The Works of Shakespeare. In which the Beauties observed by Pope, Warburton, and Dodd are pointed out. 8 vols. Edinburgh: A. Donaldson, 1771. (Boswell's only part in this work was the dedication to David Garrick.)

Reflections on the Late Alarming Bankruptcies in Scotland. Edinburgh: n.p., 1772. (A political pamphlet.)

Decision of the Court of Session on Literary Property. Edinburgh: Alexander Donaldson, 1774. (A political pamphlet.)

A Letter to the People of Scotland on the Present State of the Nation. Edinburgh: Alexander Donaldson, 1783. (A political pamphlet.)

Ode by Dr. Samuel Johnson to Mrs. Thrale, Upon Their Supposed Approaching Nuptials. London: R. Faulder, 1784. (This coarse, inexplicable performance is by Boswell, not Johnson.)

A Letter to the People of Scotland on the Alarming Attempt to Infringe the Articles of Union, and Introduce a Most Pernicious Innovation, by diminishing the number of Lords of Session. London: Charles Dilly, 1785. (A political pamphlet.)

Journal of a Tour to the Hebrides with Samuel Johnson, LL.D. London: Charles Dilly, 1785. (There have been numerous editions of this work in many languages. The first edition was reprinted in Volume V of *The Life of Samuel Johnson, LL.D.*, ed. George Birkbeck Hill, revised by L. F. Powell, Oxford: Clarendon Press, 1934-50. The Journal as Boswell wrote it was used in the edition of F. A. Pottle and C. H. Bennett, New York: Viking Press, 1936. This was reissued as one of the Yale editions by F. A. Pottle, New York: McGraw-Hill, 1961.)

William Pitt, the Grocer of London. London: n.p., 1790. (A doggerel poem in the form of a broadside.)

The Life of Samuel Johnson, LL.D. Comprehending an Account of His Studies and Numerous Works in Chronological Order . . . the Whole Exhibiting a View of Literature and Literary Men in Great Britain for Near Half a Century during which He Flourished. 2 vols. London: Charles Dilly, 1791. (Many editions, translations, and abridgments have been issued—noteworthy: John Wilson Croker, ed., 2 vols. Boston: Carter, Hendee and Co., 1731; George Birkbeck Hill, ed., New York: Bigelow, Brown, Inc., 1921; revised, enlarged, and corrected by L. F. Powell, Oxford: Clarendon Press, 1934-50.) Each of the three editions included *The Journal of a Tour to the Hebrides*.

No Abolition of Slavery; or the Universal Empire of Love: A Poem. London: R. Faulder, 1791. (An odd combination of a love poem and an attack on the abolition movement.)

The Principal Corrections and Additions of the First Edition of Mr. Boswell's Life of Johnson. London: Charles Dilly, 1793.

2. Items Appearing in Magazines and Newspapers

"An Evening Walk in the Abbey-Church of Holyroodhouse," *Scots Magazine*, XX (August, 1758), 420.

"On Hearing that the Celebrated Mr. Theophilus Cibber, Comedian, was Drowned in his passage to Ireland," *Scots Magazine*, XX (November, 1758), 587.

"Marriage between a beautiful young lady and a coarse hulk of a Gentleman," *Scots Magazine*, XX (November, 1785), 587.

"Prologue at the Opening of the Theatre Royal in Edinburgh," *Scots Magazine*, XXIX (November, 1767), 599. (This item appeared more than once in each of several periodicals.)

"On the Profession of a Player," a series of three essays in the *London Magazine*, XXXIX (August, September, October, 1770), 397-99; 468-71; 513-17. (See next section of Bibliography for modern reprints.)

"A Sketch of the Constitution of the Church of Scotland, and the State of the Parties in it at present, with specimens of Oratory of Some of the Most distinguished Members of that Church now Living," *Scots Magazine*, XXXIV (April, 1772), 187-96.

"Some Accounts of the Travels of Mr. Bruce," *Scots Magazine*, XXXII (September, 1774), 429-31, 466-71.

"Some Account of the very extraordinary Travels of the celebrated Mr. Bruce," *London Magazine*, XLIII (August, September, 1774), 388-91.

"The Hypochondriack," a series of seventy essays, *London Magazine*, XVI-LXX (October, 1777—August, 1783). (See next section of Bibliography for modern editions of these essays.)

"Observations and Reflections of John Gillie's History of Greece," *Gentleman's Magazine*, LVI (March, 1786), 237.

"Epitaph Prepared for a creature not quite dead yet," *Gentleman's Magazine*, LVI (August, 1786).

"Memoirs of James Boswell, Esq." *European Magazine*, XIX (June, 1791), 323-26, 404-7. (See next section of Bibliography for modern edition.)

3. Modern Editions of Journals, Periodical Essays, Letters, etc.

Boswelliana: The Commonplace Book of James Boswell. With a Memoir and Annotations by the Reverend Charles Rogers, LL.D. London: The Grampian Club, 1874. (Memoir of two hundred pages, composed mainly from information found in Boswell's letters to Temple. First sustained account of Boswell's life and career.)

Boswell's Notebook 1776-1777. Recording Particulars of Johnson's Early Life Communicated to Him and Others in Those Years. London: Humphrey Milford, 1925. (Arrangements of excerpts from Boswell's notes and their later forms in the first edition of the *Life*. Foreshadows subsequent discoveries relating to Boswell's artistry made possible through use of the Boswell Papers.)

The Hypochrondriack. Two editions by Margery Bailey: *The Hypochondriack*, 2 vols. Stanford: Stanford University Press, 1928, and *Boswell's Column*, London: William Kimber, 1951.

Letters of James Boswell Addressed to the Rev. W. J. Temple. Now Published from the Original Manuscript. London: Richard Bentley, 1757. Another edition (with selections from the Erskine Correspondence subjoined) by Thomas Seccombe, London: Sidgwick and Jackson, 1908.

Letters of James Boswell. Ed. C. B. Tinker. 2 vols. Oxford: The Clarendon Press, 1924.

Memoirs of James Boswell, Esq. printed in Frederick A. Pottle's *The Literary Career of James Boswell, Esq. Being the Bibliographical Materials for a Life of Boswell.* Oxford: Oxford University Press, 1929, pp. xxxix-xliv.

The Private Papers of James Boswell. 18 vols. Geoffrey Scott, editor, Vols. I-VI; Frederick A. Pottle, editor, Vols. VII-XVIII. Privately printed. Mount Vernon: W. E. Rudge, 1928-33.

The Yale Editions, listed chronologically, of the Private Papers of James Boswell:

London Journal, 1762-1763. Ed. Frederick A. Pottle. New York: McGraw-Hill, 1950.

Boswell in Holland, 1763-1764. Ed. Frederick A. Pottle. New York: McGraw-Hill, 1952.

Boswell on the Grand Tour: Germany and Switzerland, 1764. Ed. Frederick A. Pottle. New York: McGraw-Hill, 1953.

Boswell on the Grand Tour: Italy, Corsica, and France, 1765-1766. Eds. Frank Brady and Frederick A. Pottle. New York: McGraw-Hill, 1955.

Boswell in Search of a Wife, 1766-1769. Eds. Frank Brady and Frederick A. Pottle. New York: McGraw-Hill, 1956.

Boswell for the Defence, 1769-1774. Eds. William K. Wimsatt, Jr., and Frederick A. Pottle. New York: McGraw-Hill, 1959.

Journal of a Tour to the Hebrides. Edited from the original manuscript by Frederick A. Pottle and Charles H. Bennett in 1936. Reissued as one of the Yale editions, with additional notes by Professor Pottle. New

York: McGraw-Hill, 1961.

Boswell: The Ominous Years, 1774-1776. Eds. Charles Ryskamp and
Frederick A. Pottle. New York: McGraw-Hill, 1963.

Boswell in Extremes, 1776-1778. Eds. Charles McC. Weis and Frederick
A. Pottle. New York: McGraw-Hill, 1970.

Portraits by Sir Joshua Reynolds. Ed. F. W. Hilles. Issued as one of the
Yale Editions of the Private Papers of James Boswell. New York:
McGraw-Hill, 1952.

Two Research Editions of the Private Papers have been published:

Volume I: *The Correspondence of James Boswell and John Johnston of
Grange.* Ed. Ralph S. Walker. New York: McGraw-Hill, 1966.

Volume II: *The Correspondence of James Boswell Relating to the Making
of the Life of Johnson.* Ed. Marchal Waingrow. New York: McGraw-
Hill, 1969.

On the Profession of a Player. Series of three essays in the *London Magazine*, August, September, October, 1770 (XXXIX), reprinted, London:
Matthews and Marrot, 1929. The first of the three also appeared in
The English Dramatic Critics, 1660-1932 (New York: Hill and Wang,
1932), pp. 51-54.

4. *Bibliographies*

ABBOTT, CLAUDE C. A *Catalogue of Papers Relating to Boswell, Found at
Fettercairn House.* Oxford: The University Press, 1936.

ISHAM, RALPH HEYWARD. *Catalogue of an Exhibition of the Private Papers
of James Boswell, from Malahide Castle.* New York: W. E. Rudge,
1930.

POTTLE, FREDERICK A. *The Literary Career of James Boswell, Esq.* Oxford:
The Clarendon Press, 1929.

SECONDARY SOURCES

1. *Criticisms*

BAILEY, MARGERY. Introductions to two editions of the "Hypochondriack"
essays. See above, p. 169. Valuable discussions of Boswell as a periodical
essayist. Efforts to represent periods of development of his prose style,
however, not very successful.

BRADY, FRANK. *Boswell's Political Career.* New Haven: Yale University
Press, 1965. Substantial treatment of this phase of Boswell's career.
Seems mistaken, however, in the conclusion that Boswell, despite much
sound and fury, actually believed that he was parliamentary material.

BRONSON, BERTRAND H. *Johnson Agonistes and Other Essays.* Cambridge:
Cambridge University Press, 1946. One of three essays in the book,
"Boswell's Boswell," shows Bronson to be one of a small confraternity
of men who have really read the Boswell Papers. Good in discussion of
Boswell's double-consciousness.

BUTT, JOHN. *Biography in the Hands of Walton, Johnson, and Boswell.* Ewing Lectures. Los Angeles: University of California Press, 1966. An attempt to point out not so much the differences but the similarities of these three biographers, particularly in their attention to telling detail.

CARLYLE, THOMAS. "Boswell's Life of Johnson." *Critical and Miscellaneous Essays.* 4 vols. in 2 Vol. II, pp. 49-104. London: Chapman and Hall, 1888. Reprinted in *Macaulay's and Carlyle's Essays on Samuel Johnson.* Ed. William Strunk, Jr. New York: H. Holt and Company, 1895. Almost damned Boswell with much praise as one who found his hero and reverenced him. Much emphasis upon his intelligence and insight, which went beyond the reaches of logic.

CHAPMAN, R. W. *Johnsonian and Other Essays and Reviews.* Oxford: Clarendon Press, 1953. Contains a helpful discussion of the Boswell Papers.

——. *Two Centuries of Johnsonian Scholarship.* Glasgow: University of Glasgow Press, 1945. Not a compendium of scholarship, as the title might suggest, but a remarkably balanced view of Boswell, laying stress upon his exceptional vigor, industry, and genius.

CLIFFORD, JAMES L. *Young Sam Johnson.* New York: McGraw-Hill, 1955. Indispensable in any consideration of what Boswell was unable to write about Johnson's early life.

COLLINS, P. A. W. *James Boswell. Writers and their Works.* The British Council and The National Book League. London: Longmans, Green, 1956. Noteworthy for the extensive use the author made of the Boswell Papers in arriving at conclusions about Boswell's personality and art.

COPELAND, THOMAS W. "Boswell's Portrait of Burke." *The Age of Johnson. Essays Presented to Chauncey Brewster Tinker.* New Haven: Yale University Press, 1949. About Boswell's cool relationship with this great member of the Literary Club.

DANKERT, CLYDE E. "Adam Smith and James Boswell," *Queen's Quarterly,* LXVIII (1961), 323-32. Traces associations of these two Scotsmen, observing that one can learn something of Smith in Boswell's writings but nothing of Boswell in Smith's writings.

DAVIS, BERTRAM HYLTON. *Johnson Before Boswell, A Study of Sir John Hawkins' Life of Samuel Johnson.* New Haven: Yale University Press, 1960. Effort to set the record straight about Hawkins, whose biography of Johnson, it was concluded, is in some respects superior to Boswell's.

FITZGERALD, PERCY H. *Boswell's Autobiography.* London: Chatto and Windus, 1912. Development of the idea that the *Life* is actually the story of Boswell, who in leveling down Johnson built up himself.

——. *The Life of James Boswell.* 2 vols. New York: D. Appleton and Company, 1891. Most substantial book on Boswell's life and career befor the work of Pottle and his associates. Points out Boswell's self-revelations in the *Life* as a new subject for Boswellians to explore.

FUSSELL, PAUL, JR. "The Force of Literary Memory in Boswell's *London Journal*," *Studies in English Literature,* II (1962), 351-57. Considers Boswell's large store of memorized passages from literature to be of organic artistic value in the writing of the *London Journal.*

GOLDEN, JAMES L. "James Boswell on Rhetoric and Belles Lettres," *Quarterly Journal of Speech,* L (October, 1964), 266-76. Discussion of Boswell's ideas on rhetoric, literary criticism, speech content and delivery, drama, and poetry and of his performance in these areas.

GRAY, JAMES. "Boswell's Brother Confessor, William Johnson Temple," *Tennessee Studies in Literature,* IV (1959). Valuable mainly for what it reveals of Temple, Boswell's constant friend.

GREENE, DONALD J. (See Clifford, James L. and Donald J. Green, below p. 175.)

HART, FRANCIS R. "Boswell and the Romantics, a Chapter in the History of Biographical Theory," *Journal of English Literary History,* XXVII (March, 1960), 44-65. Illuminating study of Boswell's place in the development of biographical writing; emphasizes that the *Life of Johnson* was itself a mode of expression.

HOOVER, ANDREW G. "Boswell's First London Visit," *The Virginia Quarterly,* XXIX (Spring, 1953), 242-56. Contains a newly discovered, heretofore unpublished letter from Boswell to Dalrymple, purporting to tell us a little more about Boswell's somewhat obscure first London visit in 1760.

JACK, IAN. "Two Biographers: Lockhart and Boswell." *Johnson, Boswell and Their Circle.* Oxford: The University Press, 1965. Points out that Boswell placed greater value on authenticity than did Lockhart.

KERSLAKE, JOHN. *Mr. Boswell.* London: National Portrait Gallery, 1967. Prints from an exhibition of drawings, paintings, and caricatures dealing with Boswell's life and times. Very valuable book.

LEASK, W. KEITH. *James Boswell.* New York: Charles Scribner's Sons, 1896. Unhurried, quietly humorous treatment of Boswell. Not a panegyric, but sees need to correct Macaulay's negative depiction of Johnson's biographer. A small book, one of the few written on Boswell and one of the earliest.

LEWIS, WYNDHAM. *James Boswell, Short Life.* London: Eyre and Spottiswoode, 1952. First published as *The Hooded Hawk, or the Case of Mr. Boswell.* New York: Longmans, Green, 1947. Not the fullest life of Boswell but one of the sanest yet to appear.

LONGAKER, JOHN MARK. *English Biography in the Eighteenth Century.* Philadelphia: University of Pennsylvania Press, 1931. Effort to get at Boswell from many angles. Concludes that modern biography falls short of excellent biography because it falls short of Boswell's methods.

LUSTIG, IRMA S. "Boswell's Literary Criticism in the Life of Johnson,"

Studies in English Literature 1500-1900 (Rice University), VI (1966), 529-41. Conversations, letters, and comments in the *Life* are used to show that Boswell possessed critical acumen.

McAdam, E. L. *Johnson and Boswell: A Survey of Their Writings.* Boston: Houghton Mifflin, 1969. Last third of book devoted to useful brief survey of Boswell's career.

Macaulay, Thomas Babington. *Miscellaneous Works of Lord Macaulay.* Ed. Lady Trevelyan. 8 vols. London: Longmans, 1880. Review of Croker's edition of the *Life of Johnson*: Vol. I, pp. 581f.; "Essay on Johnson": Vol. IV, pp. 56f. (first published in *Encyclopaedia Britannica*, 1856). Potent force in furtherance of the paradoxical view that the *Life of Johnson* issued from an insufferable ass who was not conscious of his art.

McLaren, Moray. *Corsica Boswell: Paoli, Johnson and Freedom.* London: Secker and Warburg, 1966. Used Boswell's experiences and observations on the Corsica journey as backdrops for his own as he made the same journey. Boswell's Corsica *Tour* reprinted here.

————. *The Highland Jaunt. A Study of James Boswell and Samuel Johnson Upon Their Highland and Hebridean Tour of 1773.* London: Jarrolds, 1954. A valuable companion to Boswell's Hebrides Journal. Done by a Scotsman who followed Johnson and Boswell's trail and collected background information on places, persons, and historical events.

Mallory, George. *Boswell the Biographer.* London: Smith, Elder and Company. 1912. Points out differences between Boswell's manner in the *Tour* and that in the *Life*. Attributes Boswell's supremacy to his knowing "most intimately" the man he was portraying.

Maurois, André. *Aspects of Biography.* Translated from the French by S. C. Roberts. Cambridge: Cambridge University Press, 1929. Points out essential difference between the nature of biographical truth as pursued by Boswell and the more complex truth that is the object of some modern biographers.

Nicolson, Harold. *The Development of English Biography.* London: Hogarth Press, 1933. Shows more contempt for Boswell as a person than Macaulay did; but, unlike Macaulay, perceives the artist at work in his combining of methods used by other biographers. Holds that only a special talent, but not genius, required for biography.

Pearson, Hesketh. *Johnson and Boswell—the Story of Their Lives.* New York: Harper's, 1959 (published preceding year in London). Great deal of Bozzy, but nothing of any value about him as a writer.

Pottle, Frederick A. "Boswell Revalued." *Literary Views: Critical and Historical Essays.* Published for Rice University. Chicago: University of Chicago Press, 1964. Points up fact that the literary world is now able (after discovery of Boswell Papers) to view Boswell's Journal as his unique performance.

————— "Bozzy and Yorick," *Blackwood's Magazine*, CCXVII (March, 1925), 298-313. Brings forward evidence to show that Boswell on his first visit to London (1760) did some hobnobbing with Laurence Sterne.

————— "The Incredible Boswell," *Blackwood's Magazine*, CCXVIII (August, 1925), 149-56. Account of Boswell's amazine journalistic activities in connection with Corsica and the Douglas case; discovered by examining Boswell's marked file of the *London Chronicle* for 1767-1775.

————— *James Boswell: The Earlier Years, 1740-1769*. New York: McGraw-Hill, 1966. The first volume of the long-awaited definitive biography of Boswell.

————— "The Life of Boswell," *Yale Review*, XXXV (1945-46), 444-60. Written shortly before Professor Pottle announced work in progress on his biography of Boswell. Holds that the "Boswellian paradox" created by Macaulay must give way to the facts now available in the Boswell Papers and to the proper use of the facts.

QUENNELL, PETER. *The Profane Virtues: Four Studies of the Eighteenth Century*. New York: The Viking Press, 1945. Studies of Boswell, Gibbon, Sterne, and Wilkes. Good use of the Boswell Papers in providing a lively account of the highlights of Boswell's life, but very little said about his literary career.

RALEIGH, WALTER. *Six Essays on Johnson*. Oxford: The Clarendon Press, 1910. Wary of giving Boswell too much credit for the image of the great Johnson; ready to admit, however, that Boswell's Johnson is the Johnson we know best.

ROBERTS, S. C. *Doctor Johnson and Others*. Cambridge: Cambridge University Press, 1958. One chapter devoted to an interesting comparison between the two diarists Boswell and Pepys.

SALTPETER, HARRY. *Dr. Johnson & Boswell*. New York: Coward-McCann, 1929. Had access to the first six volumes of the Private Papers in presenting a flesh-and-blood Boswell. Very little notice of his literary career, however, or of him as writer of his own life.

SCOTT, GEOFFREY. *The Making of the Life of Johnson as Shown in Boswell's First Notes*. Volume VI *of The Private Papers of James Boswell*. 18 vols. Eds. Geoffrey Scott (Vol. I-VI) and Frederick A. Pottle (Vol. VII-XVIII). Privately printed. Mount Vernon: W. E. Rudge, 1928-34. Indispensable for a study of Boswell's art in the writing of Johnson's conversation.

TINKER, CHAUNCEY BREWSTER. *Young Boswell: Chapters on James Boswell the Biographer*. Boston: *The Atlantic Monthly* Press 1922. Based on the heretofore unstudied manuscripts of the Temple letters. A fine appreciation of Boswell before availability of the Boswell Papers.

VULLIAMY, C. E. *James Boswell*. New York: Charles Scribner's Sons 1933. Almost violent denigration. No accounting for the great biography from a man who, after all, was quite mad.

WAINGROW, MARSHALL. See Research Editions of the Private Papers, above, p. 170.

WALKER, RALPH S. See Research Editions of the Private Papers, above, p. 170.

WIMSATT, WILLIAM K. JR. "James Boswell: the Man and the Journal," *Yale Review*, XLIX (Autumn, 1959), 80-92. One of the most penetrating and sensitive appreciations of Boswell's Journals as literature. Literature *as journal* and literature *as narrative,* in which Boswell is a hero such as one finds in good fiction.

2. Bibliographies

BROWN, ANTHONY E. *Boswellian Studies: A Bibliography. Cairo Studies in English,* ed. Magdi Wahba (1963-66), pp. 1-75. Cairo: Anglo-Egyptian Bookshop, 1966. Longest list of studies on Boswell yet to appear.

CLIFFORD, JAMES L. *Johnsonian Studies, 1887-1950: A Survey and Bibliography.* Minneapolis: University of Minnesota Press, 1951. Good bibliography of Boswell in this and following work. Limited, however, to works and events connected with Johnson.

CLIFFORD, JAMES L. and DONALD J. GREENE. *A Bibliography of Johnsonian Studies. Johnsonian Studies.* Ed. Magdi Wahba. Cairo: Anglo-Egyptian Bookshop, 1962. (See entry above.)

Index